Reptiles
and
Amphibians

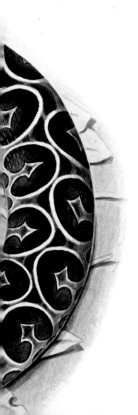

LiTTLE GUiDES

Reptiles
and
Amphibians

Consultant Editor
Dr Mark Hutchinson

FOG CITY PRESS

Published by Fog City Press
814 Montgomery Street
San Francisco, CA 94133 USA

Copyright © 2006 Weldon Owen Inc.
First printed 2006

Chief Executive Officer: John Owen
President: Terry Newell
Publisher: Sheena Coupe
Creative Director: Sue Burk
Project Management: Limelight Press Pty Ltd
Project Editor: John Mapps
Series Design: Nika Markovtzev
Project Designer: Jacqueline Richards
Editorial Coordinator: Helen Flint
Production Director: Chris Hemesath
Production Coordinator: Charles Mathews
Sales Manager: Emily Bartle
Vice President International Sales: Stuart Laurence
Administrator International Sales: Kristine Ravn

ISBN 1-74089-545-2

Color reproduction by SC (Sang Choy) International Pte Ltd
Printed by SNP Leefung Printers Ltd
Printed in China

A Weldon Owen Production
Produced using arkiva retrieval technology
For further information, contact arkiva@weldonowen.com.au

Contents

INTRODUCING REPTILES
AND AMPHIBIANS

What Are Reptiles?

Reptiles are vertebrates (animals with a backbone) that have a body covered in tough scales. They are ectotherms, which means that they get their body heat from outside sources, for example, by basking in the sun. Most are not "cold blooded" as the old expression goes—when active, they can be as warm as any bird or mammal. Reptiles come in many different shapes and sizes, and live in most habitats, from the oceans to the deserts. Alligators, crocodiles, snakes, lizards, turtles, and tortoises are all reptiles.

Crocodile

REPTILES IN DANGER

Sea turtle numbers are declining because people catch them in fishing nets or steal their eggs. The Pacific hawksbill turtle is an endangered species.

TYPES OF REPTILES
The reptile world is made up of four groups called orders. The orders are crocodiles and alligators, turtles and tortoises, lizards and snakes, and the lizard-like tuataras.

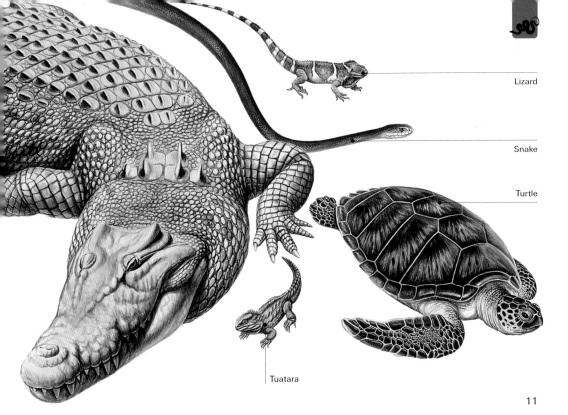

Lizard

Snake

Turtle

Tuatara

11

What Are Amphibians?

The word amphibian comes from a Greek word that means "a being with a double life." Most amphibians live two different lives—in water as larvae and on land as adults. But some live their whole lives in water and others never leave land. Like reptiles, they are ectothermic, but unlike reptiles, most are active at much lower body temperatures, and they have moist skins rather than a covering of scales. The three groups of amphibians are frogs and toads, salamanders and newts, and wormlike caecilians. There are about 4,950 species of living amphibians.

DID YOU KNOW?

The vast majority of amphibians are active only during the night.

FROGS AND TOADS
Frogs and toads are the most numerous and diverse of the amphibians. They have bulging eyes and large back legs. Most live in or near water. This glass frog lives in trees above streams in American rain forests.

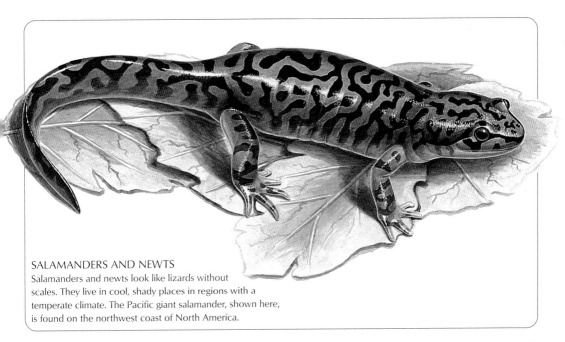

SALAMANDERS AND NEWTS
Salamanders and newts look like lizards without
scales. They live in cool, shady places in regions with a
temperate climate. The Pacific giant salamander, shown here,
is found on the northwest coast of North America.

Skin and Scales

The skin of most amphibians is thin
and needs to be kept moist to work
properly. This skin allows water to be absorbed or
lost, and lets oxygen into the body. Reptiles have tough,
dry skins covered with scales. The scales act as protection
against predators, stop the animal drying out when water is
scarce, and absorb heat to keep the animal warm. Reptiles shed
their scales to keep their skin in good condition. Some, including
crocodiles and turtles, shed individual scales, while snakes and
lizards shed the outer layer of their scales as a sheet several
times a year.

DID YOU KNOW?

**File snakes have scales like
sandpaper to help them grip
slippery fish.**

OFF WITH THE OLD SKIN
This American copperhead snake is wriggling free of its dry, old skin, which comes away in one piece.

Body Temperature

Reptiles have warm bodies when they are active, like mammals and birds. Reptiles get their body heat from the sun, either by basking or moving into warm areas. To cool down during the hottest part of the day, reptiles expose as little of their body as possible to the sun's rays, or they move into the shade.

TEMPERATURE CONTROL
A lizard adopts different positions to warm up or cool down.

WARMING UP
After swimming in cold water, this marine iguana warms itself by basking in the sun.

16

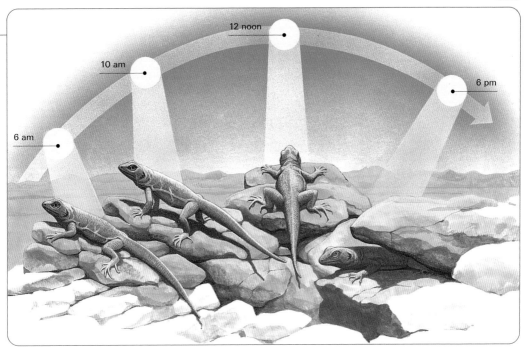

6 am

10 am

12 noon

6 pm

The Need for Water

Water is very important for amphibians because most species lay their eggs in it, and all must keep their skin moist. This means that the majority of amphibians live in moist or humid environments. Species that spend a long time in water have bodies suited to an aquatic life. Salamanders, for example, have paddle-like tails for swimming, while frogs that live in water have webbed toes for the same reason.

WATER WORLD
Frogs and toads can be found in nearly all habitats, but most live in water for at least part of their lives. Nearly all frogs can swim, though some are better at it than others.

DID YOU KNOW?

The water-holding frog of Australia survives droughts underground in a cocoon.

POND LIFE
The mudpuppy lives all its life in North American lakes, ponds, rivers, and streams. Like a fish, it breathes through gills. These are red and bushy.

New Life

Most reptiles and amphibians lay eggs. Reptile embryos develop inside eggs with enough yolk to grow into miniature versions of the adult. Amphibians have a two-stage life cycle. Their eggs have only a small amount of yolk, but hatch into water-living larvae, such as tadpoles, which are often very different from an adult. The larvae change into adults that breathe air and live mostly on land.

HARD SHELL

A reptile embryo develops in a hard, waterproof shell.

JELLY CAPSULE

An amphibian embryo is surrounded by dense jelly.

FULLY FORMED

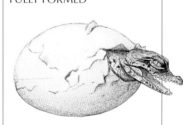

A reptile emerges from its egg as a miniature adult.

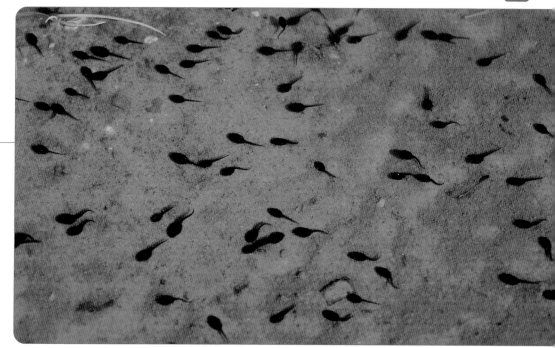

ORIGINS OF
REPTILES AND
AMPHIBIANS

The First Amphibians

The first amphibians came into existence about 360 million years ago. They evolved from lobe-finned fish, which had lungs and large fins, and could live on land for short periods of time. Amphibians developed into many different forms. Just like today, some of them spent most of their time in water, while others were land dwellers.

FISH OUT OF WATER
This lobe-finned fish, *Eusthenopteron*, lived about 400 million years ago.

EARLY AMPHIBIAN
Ichthyostega was one of the earliest amphibians. It lived about 360 million years ago.

The First Reptiles

About 50 million years after the first amphibians appeared, the first reptiles evolved from an amphibian ancestor. The earliest reptiles looked like small lizards. A hundred million years later, reptiles had replaced amphibians as the dominant land animals. Early reptiles developed into the first dinosaurs, which dominated the land, and into a range of other reptiles that flew in the skies and swam in the seas.

EARLY REPTILE
The earliest known reptile is
Hylonomus, which was about
8 inches (20 cm) long.

DID YOU KNOW?

The earliest reptiles probably hunted and fed on insects.

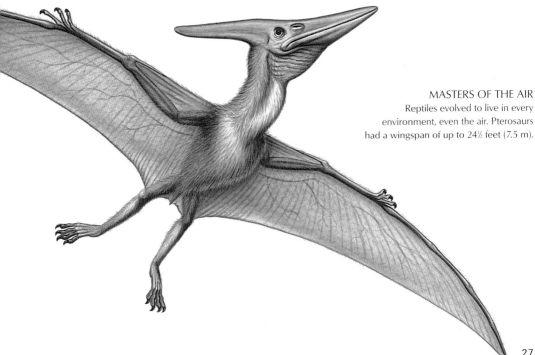

MASTERS OF THE AIR
Reptiles evolved to live in every
environment, even the air. Pterosaurs
had a wingspan of up to 24½ feet (7.5 m).

The Age of Reptiles

From 250 to 65 million years ago, reptiles dominated the land, sea, and sky. As well as dinosaurs, there were ocean-going plesiosaurs, flying pterosaurs, lizards, snakes, crocodiles, turtles, and tuataras. All large reptiles, except crocodiles and turtles, became extinct about 65 million years ago, but the ancestors of today's reptiles survived to evolve into thousands of different species.

REPTILES RULE
Prehistoric reptiles ranged from small turtles and flying lizards to gigantic dinosaurs such as the *Stegosaurus* (far right) and creatures with a "sail" on their back.

28

Dinosaur Diversity

The first dinosaurs appeared 228 million years ago. A huge number of dinosaur types developed from them—we know of at least 1,000 different ones. Some were the size of chickens. Others were the biggest meat-eaters the world has known, such as the 46 foot (14 m) *Tyrannosaurus*. Still others were plant-eating giants: *Saltasaurus* reached 39 feet (12 m) in length, and *Triceratops* was about 30 feet (9 m) long.

CRETACEOUS PARADE
Dinosaurs were at their most varied and numerous during the Cretaceous period, between 165 and 145 million years ago.

SMALL BEGINNINGS

Like the reptiles of today, dinosaurs laid eggs.

Triceratops

Corythosaurus

Tyrannosaurus

Saltasaurus

Euoplocephalus

Pachycephalosaurus

Ancient Marine Reptiles

While dinosaurs ruled the land, their cousin reptiles dominated the sea. The oceans were home to plesiosaurs, pliosaurs, ichthyosaurs, marine turtles, crocodiles, and other reptiles. Plesiosaurs had long necks and ate small creatures. Pliosaurs had large heads and short necks, and tackled larger prey with their strong teeth and claws. Ichthyosaurs had streamlined bodies and sharklike fins and a tail.

The pliosaur *Peloneustes* was 10 feet (3 m) long.

Nothosaurus was 10 feet (3 m) long.

MARINE MASTERS
The oceans were full of marine reptiles of many different shapes and sizes. They competed to feed on fish, small sea creatures, and each other.

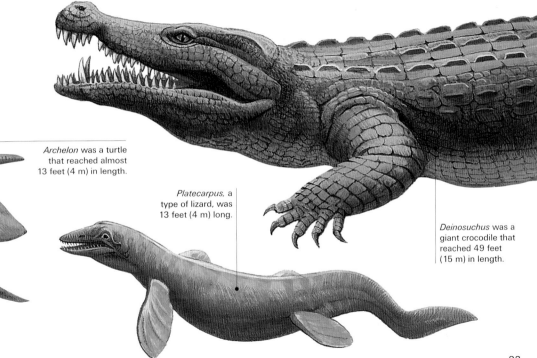

Archelon was a turtle that reached almost 13 feet (4 m) in length.

Platecarpus, a type of lizard, was 13 feet (4 m) long.

Deinosuchus was a giant crocodile that reached 49 feet (15 m) in length.

ALL ABOUT
REPTILES

Turtles and Tortoises

Turtles and tortoises are known as chelonians. They are the only reptiles that have a shell built into the skeleton. Like other reptiles, they lay eggs. Most turtles live in water, but tortoises are land dwellers. Sea turtles live in the oceans. Freshwater turtles occur in ponds, lakes, streams, and rivers. All sea turtles and some freshwater turtles leave the water only to lay eggs. Other species move between water and land. Land tortoises live in dry areas where there are no open bodies of water.

> DID YOU KNOW?
>
> **The smallest chelonian is the speckled padloper. It is only 3¼ inches (95 mm) long.**

A REAL STINKER

The southern loggerhead musk turtle lives in fresh water in southern North America. When disturbed, these turtles release a very strong smell.

BRIGHT BOY

This male painted turtle has a brightly colored shell, head, and legs. It lives in ponds and rivers in North America and has a 10 inch (25 cm) long shell.

BEAUTIFULLY MARKED

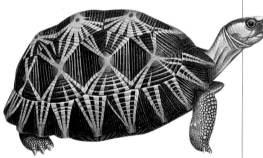

The shell of the radiated tortoise has beautiful markings. This land tortoise is found in dry regions of southwest Madagascar, where it is endangered.

Chelonians Up Close

The shells of chelonians set them apart from all other reptiles. The shell consists of two parts: the upper part is called the carapace, and the lower part is the plastron. Each part has an inner bony layer and an outer layer of horny plates (scutes). Chelonians are divided into two groups according to the way they draw their head into their shell. One group has a flexible neck that can be pulled back straight into the shell. The members of the other group bend their neck sideways and curl their head under the front of their upper shell. Either method protects the chelonian from enemies.

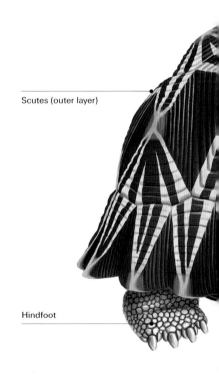

Scutes (outer layer)

Hindfoot

INSIDE THE SHELL
The shell is attached to the spine and ribs. Scutes make up the shell's outer layer; a bony layer lies underneath. The flexible neck bones allow the animal to draw its head into its shell.

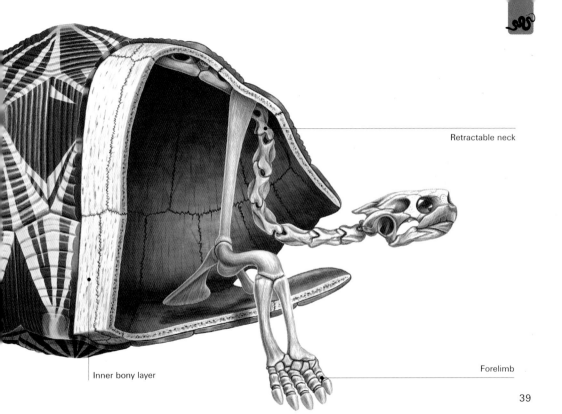

Retractable neck

Inner bony layer

Forelimb

Shell Shapes

SEMI-TERRESTRIAL TURTLE
Semi-terrestrial (semi-land) turtles divide their time between
the land and the water. Their shells are not as high as those
of land tortoises, but not as flat as those of sea turtles.

SEA TURTLE
Sea turtles are fast swimmers in the oceans, and come
ashore only to lay eggs. They have light shells that are
streamlined to make swimming easier.

LAND TORTOISE
Land tortoises have thick, dome-shaped shells for protection from predators. As their shells are very strong and heavy, land tortoises move slowly.

POND TURTLE
Pond turtles spend most of their time in small bodies of fresh water. They have small, flattened, usually lighter shells, to make swimming easier.

Suitable Limbs

The legs of turtles and tortoises have evolved to suit the different environments in which they live. Land tortoises have column-shaped legs with large claws to grip the earth. Pond turtles need to move on land and in the water, so they have webbing between their claws. Sea turtles have large front flippers to push them quickly through the water.

FAST SWIMMERS
Sea turtles are built for life in the oceans. As well as large front flippers, they have light, streamlined shells. On land, however, they are clumsy and have to drag themselves along.

LAND TORTOISE
Column-shaped legs; large claws

POND TURTLE
Webbing between the claws

SEA TURTLE
Legs have evolved into flippers.

Turtle Love

Mating behavior varies from the male simply mounting the female, to elaborate courtship rituals. Courtship in tortoises usually involves some head-bobbing, with the male head-butting and biting the female.

MATING TIME
Sea turtles mate for the first time when they are several years old, then return to the same beach to breed.

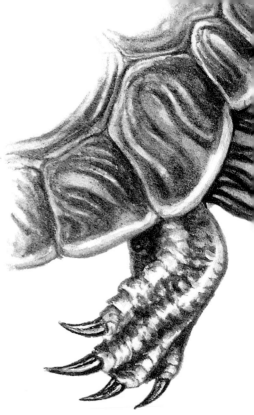

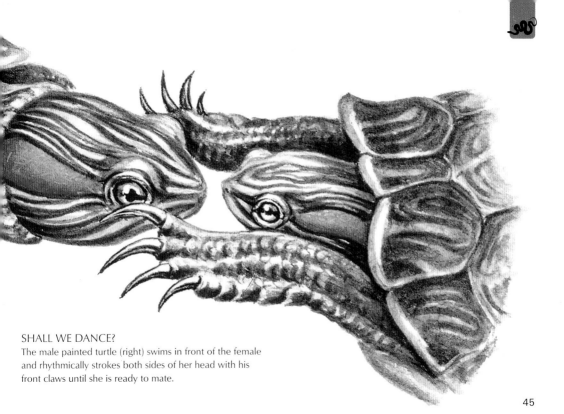

SHALL WE DANCE?

The male painted turtle (right) swims in front of the female and rhythmically strokes both sides of her head with his front claws until she is ready to mate.

Fending for Themselves

After mating, turtles and tortoises lay their eggs in shallow
burrows, usually near the areas where they live and feed.
Females lay the eggs and cover the nest. The eggs of most
species hatch after a few months. In many species, the
hatchlings spend the winter in the egg chamber and come
outside during the spring. After the eggs are laid, the parents
show no further interest in the young. From the day they
leave the nest, the hatchlings must fend for themselves.

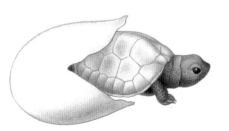

LAYING EGGS
Land tortoises lay their eggs
in nests scraped out of the
soil, burying them afterward.
Burying the eggs keeps them
at a constant temperature.

INDEPENDENCE DAY
Chelonians are independent from the moment they leave the egg.

ON ITS OWN

A newly hatched sea turtle makes its way to the ocean. With no protection from their parents, many hatchlings are killed by predators such as birds.

Feeding Time

Sea turtles eat shellfish, fish, jellyfish, and sea grasses. Semi-terrestrial turtles hunt on land and water, and eat both plant and animal food. Young land tortoises eat worms and insects as well as plants. Adult land tortoises, which move too slowly to catch animals, eat flowers, fruits, and plants.

SHARP JAWS
Turtles and tortoises, such as this giant land tortoise, do not have teeth. They use their sharp-edged jaws to grasp and cut plant and animal food.

BERRY TREAT
This eastern box turtle is just about to devour some wild strawberries. As well as plants, it eats snails, slugs, insects, and earthworms.

WORMS FOR VARIETY
A wood turtle makes a meal of an earthworm. These turtles venture short distances from their watery homes to find food, which includes both plants and animals.

In and Out of Water

Most turtles and tortoises live in or near fresh water such as lakes, rivers, and swamps. Almost all freshwater turtles have webbed feet with claws, and light, flat shells. To feed, they lie underwater, waiting for their prey of insects and fish to come past. Hunting on land and in the water, semi-terrestrial turtles eat various plants and small animals. In winter, some of them hibernate in mud under water or in burrows on land.

GONE FISHING
An American snapping turtle snaps up a fish. This species spends most of its time in water.

INTO THE TREES
The big-headed turtle of Vietnam is a poor swimmer. It is a good climber, however, and can sometimes be seen soaking up the sun on the branches of trees and bushes.

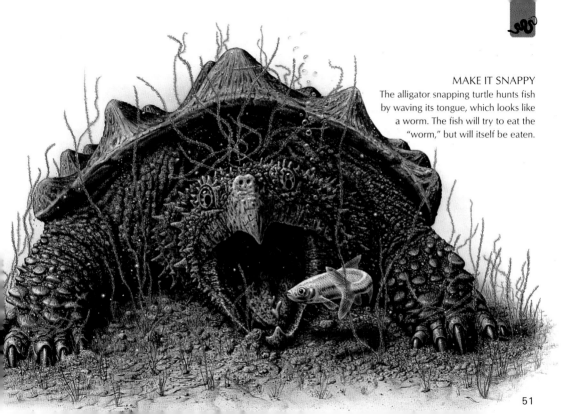

MAKE IT SNAPPY
The alligator snapping turtle hunts fish by waving its tongue, which looks like a "worm." The fish will try to eat the "worm," but will itself be eaten.

Land Tortoises—Little and Large

There are about 40 species of land tortoises. Many of them live in dry environments or deserts. Most have high-domed shells to protect them from predators. As their shells are strong and heavy, land tortoises move slowly. Most species are plant-eaters, though some also eat insects.

HEAVYWEIGHT
Galápagos tortoises weigh between 330 and 440 pounds (150–200 kg).

SIZE RANGE
At just over 3 inches (8 cm) long, the speckled padloper is the world's smallest land tortoise. Other land tortoises shown here range in size from the 4 inch (10 cm) long Madagascan spider tortoises to the 8 inch (20 cm) long South American tortoises and the wheelbarrow-sized giants of the Aldabra and Galápagos islands.

Keeping Cool

Many land tortoises live in hot, dry areas of the world, such as deserts. In these places, tortoises have to be careful not to overheat or dry out. They are active only during the coolest times of the day—the morning and the late afternoon or evening. During the hottest part of the day, they lie in the shade of shrubs and trees or in burrows in the soil.

TUCKED IN
As well as keeping cool, turtles and tortoises must keep moist. The ornate box turtle draws its head and legs into its domed shell to protect itself from drying out and from predators.

COOL HOME
The gopher tortoise of North America lives in deserts. Active in the early morning and evening, it digs a burrow and retreats into it during the hottest part of the day. The burrow can also be used to keep warm in winter.

Galápagos Giants

Giant tortoises live on the Galápagos Islands in the Pacific Ocean. Those on the large, wetter islands have developed big dome-like shells. Tortoises on the smaller, drier islands where plants grow tall have long legs and a smaller shell called a saddleback. This shell is raised in front so that the tortoises can stretch their neck and reach up to the plants.

SADDLEBACK STRETCH
In dry times, giant saddleback tortoises get water and food from tall cactus plants. When it rains, dozens of tortoises collect around puddles and drink as much as they can.

NO NEED FOR LUNCH
If necessary, Galápagos tortoises can go without food for up to a year.

Sea Turtles

Sea turtles are found in all the tropical and subtropical oceans of the world. They eat fish, jellyfish, sponges, crabs, clams, mussels, sea urchins, and marine plants such as seaweed. They use their large front limbs like paddles to move through the water. The smaller rear limbs act as rudders. Sea turtles use the ocean currents to help them search for food.

BURST OF SPEED

Sea turtles usually swim slowly, helped by currents. But they can put on a quick burst to escape from predators such as sharks, reaching speeds of up to 18 miles (29 km) per hour.

Life at Sea

Sea turtles spend almost all their life at sea. The males never leave the water and the females do so only to lay eggs. The two sexes travel vast distances across the oceans to breed. They meet at sea near the beach where the nest will be. After mating, the female comes ashore at night to lay the eggs. She lays as many as 200 of them. Many sea turtles are endangered because of hunting by humans.

DID YOU KNOW?

Sea turtles often sunbathe at the ocean surface on floating fields of seaweed.

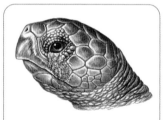

EYE WASH
Sea turtles produce "tears" from special glands close to the eyes to get rid of salt.

LONG DISTANCE
Some green turtles swim from the coast of Brazil to beaches in the mid-Atlantic to lay their eggs.

RACE FOR SURVIVAL
Newly born flatback turtles dig themselves out of the
sand and race to the sea. They stick together as a
group to try to escape being eaten by predators.

61

Softshell Turtles

Instead of a hard shell, these turtles have a leathery skin, which is light and flexible. They hide on the muddy beds of freshwater rivers, lakes, and streams, and eat mollusks, insects, crustaceans, worms, frogs, and fish.

AT HOME UNDER WATER
Softshell turtles are adapted for life in the water. As well as a light shell, they have webbed feet and snorkel-shaped snouts for breathing beneath the surface.

SPINY SHELL EDGE
The eastern spiny softshell turtle is a colorful species of southeastern North America.

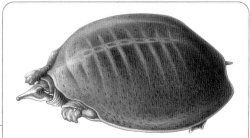

TURTLE PANCAKE
With its head and legs retracted, the smooth softshell turtle looks a bit like a pancake.

Crocodilians

Crocodiles, alligators, caimans, and gharials are known as crocodilians. Most species live in tropical parts of the world, in Asia, Africa, Australia, and the Americas. They are excellent swimmers and can also walk on land. All are stealthy predators. Among the crocodilians are some of the largest and most dangerous reptiles in the world.

Crocodilian Characteristics

Crocodilians have long, narrow bodies covered in a leathery skin. They spend much of their time in the water, where they swim using powerful bladelike tails. Crocodilians have short legs and cannot walk far on land. They have extra eyelids that are transparent, and close to keep the water out. Their large mouths have many sharp teeth for killing and tearing apart prey.

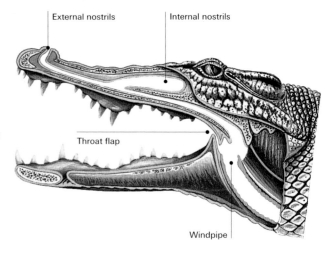

External nostrils

Internal nostrils

Throat flap

Windpipe

UNDERWATER ADAPTATIONS

A crocodilian can breathe while half under water because it has external nostrils that remain above the water. It also has a throat flap to stop water going down the windpipe when the animal is killing prey under water.

SALTWATER CROCODILE

The largest species of crocodilian is the saltwater crocodile. It can grow to 23 feet (7 m) in length.

TOMISTOMA

The tomistoma or false gharial is a medium-sized crocodilian. It reaches a length of about 13 feet (4 m).

CUVIER'S DWARF CAIMAN

This is the smallest crocodilian. It is 5 feet (1.5 m) long fully grown.

A Head and Side View

Crocodilian snouts vary in shape and size, according to their diets and the way they live. Gharials live in fast-flowing rivers and feed on fish, so their snout is narrow and full of small teeth, good for gripping fish. Alligators, caimans, and crocodiles feed on larger animals and have a big head with powerful jaws and large teeth. Alligators and caimans live in swamps with lots of vegetation. With their stronger heads and variable sized teeth, the broader-headed crocodilians can trap and hold a wide variety of prey.

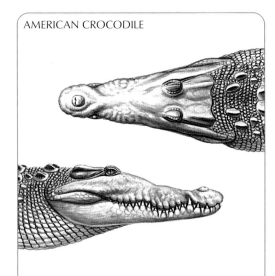

AMERICAN CROCODILE

Crocodiles' snouts are usually pointed and not as broad as those of alligators. When crocodiles close their mouth, the fourth tooth in the lower jaw is just visible.

DID YOU KNOW?

Nile crocodiles have been seen to kill fully grown Cape buffaloes.

BLACK CAIMAN

The black caiman, like other caimans and alligators, has a broad, heavy snout. When alligators and caimans close their mouth, no lower teeth can be seen.

GHARIAL

Gharials have extremely thin snouts and many small, pointed teeth. The teeth are excellent for holding on to the slippery bodies of its main prey, fish.

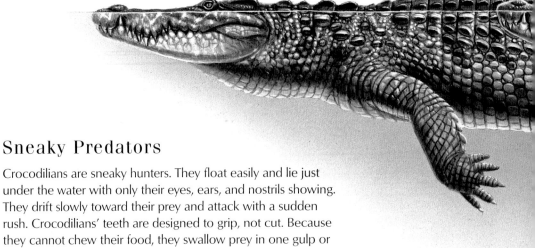

Sneaky Predators

Crocodilians are sneaky hunters. They float easily and lie just under the water with only their eyes, ears, and nostrils showing. They drift slowly toward their prey and attack with a sudden rush. Crocodilians' teeth are designed to grip, not cut. Because they cannot chew their food, they swallow prey in one gulp or tear it into large pieces.

Mother Care

Female crocodilians look after their eggs and young more carefully than most other reptiles. They lay eggs in nests or bury them in holes in the sand or soil. Many predators, including fish, lizards, mammals, birds, and sometimes even other crocodilians, would like to eat newly hatched crocodilians. The mother guards her hatchlings for several weeks or more until the young can fend for themselves.

CARRIED IN COMFORT
This hatchling alligator is being carried in its mother's mouth.

Guarding the Nest

Female crocodilians guard their nests, scaring away predators such as large lizards, mammals, and birds. The eggs take 60 to 100 days to develop, depending on the species and the temperature of the nest. The nest's temperature determines the sex of the hatchlings. The highest and lowest temperatures usually produce females, while in-between temperatures usually produce males.

PREDATOR-FREE
Young crocodiles in a crocodile farm are protected from predators.

MOTHER IS WATCHING
A female crocodile guards her nest, which is covered with warm, rotting plant material, for up to 100 days. She does not leave the nest and will attack any intruder that comes too close.

Crocodiles

There are 13 species of crocodiles. They range from medium to large, and have quite narrow snouts. Crocodiles and alligators look very similar, but you can tell them apart by looking at their teeth. The fourth tooth in a crocodile's lower jaw is still visible when the crocodile closes its mouth. All of the alligator's upper teeth fit into pits in the upper jaw and cannot be seen. Crocodiles live in a variety of freshwater and saltwater habitats, such as lagoons, swamps, beaches, and rivers, in Australia, Africa, North and South America, and Asia.

WAITING FOR PREY
A crocodile lies partly submerged, waiting for its prey. When they strike, crocodiles move quickly through the water, lunge up onto the bank and pull the prey into the water. They then drown and eat the prey.

The Crocodile Walk

Crocodiles are good swimmers and spend most of their time in water, but sometimes they must move over land. When they need to move rapidly, usually to retreat to water, they use an awkward, sprawling action. On slippery or muddy surfaces, they slide or crawl on their belly. Over long distances on dry land, a crocodile walks in a similar way to mammals. Some species can gallop quickly to escape danger.

> DID YOU KNOW?
>
> **When a crocodile gallops, all four limbs may be in the air at the same time.**

Walking involves keeping the belly well off the ground.

ON THE MOVE
Crocodiles often crawl the short distance from a muddy riverbank to the water. On dry land, they lift up their body and walk, dragging their tail. Crocodiles that can gallop, only do so for short distances.

A crocodile crawls on its belly just before entering the water.

A galloping crocodile moves like a horse at high speed.

OUT FOR A WALK
A Nile crocodile walks slowly across a mudflat toward its real home, the river.

79

Gharials

Gharials have long, narrow snouts. They feed mainly on fish, but also eat insects, frogs, snakes, and birds. There are two species. The gharial lives in fast-flowing rivers and hill streams in India, Pakistan, Bangladesh, Nepal, Bhutan, and Burma. It reaches 20 feet (6 m) in length. The tomistoma, or false gharial, inhabits freshwater lakes, swamps, and rivers in parts of Thailand, Malaysia, and Indonesia. It grows to 13 feet (4 m).

UNDER THREAT
Habitat destruction and hunting have endangered the tomistoma.

FISH-EATER
The gharial's extremely thin snout and its many small, pointed teeth are ideal for grasping the struggling, slippery bodies of fish.

80

Table Manners

Unlike other reptiles, crocodilians do not chew their food. Instead, they swallow prey whole or tear it into large pieces before swallowing. Most species swallow stones and hard objects, called gastroliths, which help to break down the food so it can be digested.

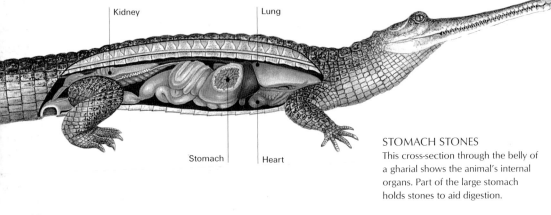

Kidney

Lung

Stomach

Heart

STOMACH STONES
This cross-section through the belly of a gharial shows the animal's internal organs. Part of the large stomach holds stones to aid digestion.

Alligators and Caimans

Alligators and their close relatives, caimans, have a broader snout than crocodiles, and grow to be almost as big. There are two species of alligators, the American alligator, which can grow to 19 feet (6 m), and the much smaller and rarer Chinese alligator. The several species of caimans live in various parts of Central and South America. The largest is the black caiman, which can reach about 16 feet (5 m) in length.

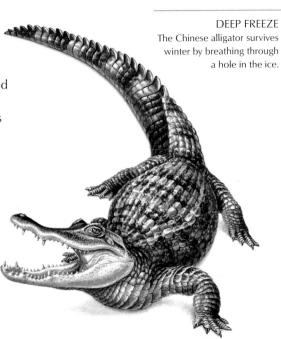

DEEP FREEZE
The Chinese alligator survives winter by breathing through a hole in the ice.

COMMON CAIMAN
The common caiman of South America grows to about 8 feet (2.5 m) in length and looks like a small crocodile. It eats insects, crabs, snails, and fish.

Jump Shot

Crocodiles and alligators rely heavily on their ability to surprise their prey by suddenly exploding into action. Most of the time, the kill takes place in or under water. But sometimes it happens in midair. If a bird comes too close to the water, a crocodile or alligator makes a jump shot, lunging upward and lifting its body almost clear of the water. Its massive jaws do the rest.

UNDERWATER HUNTER
A Johnston's crocodile puts on a burst of speed to catch fish.

LUNGE FOR LUNCH
American alligators often hunt near waterbird colonies where the birds eat the fish that gather there. Occasionally an alligator will leap from the water to catch a bird such as this egret chick, which has fallen from its nest.

DID YOU KNOW?

Two species of crocodiles attack humans: the Nile and the saltwater crocodile.

Lizards at Large

No other group of reptiles has developed into as many different forms as the lizards. They range from tiny legless wormlike creatures to giant monitors with powerful limbs.

LIZARDS OF THE SEA
Marine iguanas of the Galápagos Islands live in
large colonies throughout most of the year.

Looking at Lizards

There are about 3,750 species of lizards in the world. They come in all shapes and sizes, from a tiny gecko to the 10 foot (3 m) long Komodo dragon. Some are short and fat; others are legless and look like snakes. Some lizards are brightly colored, while others are dull and blend into the background. Most are predators, and eat everything from ants and insects to other lizards and animals as large as goats.

TINY LIZARD
Most lizards are small, which allows them to occupy numerous habitats. This tiny anole is clinging to a stem of grass.

LITTLE LEOPARD
The 8 inch (20 cm) leopard gecko gets its name from its beautifully patterned skin.

VENOMOUS MONSTER
The gila monster lives in arid regions of Mexico and the United States. It is one of only two lizards to have a venomous bite.

Lizard Bodies

Boyd's forest dragon puffs out its throat flap and shows off its scaly crests to communicate with other forest dragons.

The Argus goanna uses its tail as a prop to stand up and look around.

LOW PROFILE

A flat body helps this desert short-horned lizard hide from predators.

SNAKELIKE SHAPE

The legless lizard looks very similar to a snake. It has a streamlined body that makes it easy to move in and out of narrow places.

ATHLETIC HUNTER

A slim, athletic body makes this perentie an excellent long-distance runner.

STANDARD MODEL

A wall lizard has the most common lizard body shape.

Every Tail Tells a Story

Some lizards have tails that look like leaves; others have tails that look like heads. Both types of tails fool predators. Some tails are used to hold on to branches or to store fat. Skinks can shed their tail. If a predator grabs a skink's tail, the tail breaks off and stays in the predator's mouth while the skink escapes.

FAT TAIL
Shingleback tails store fat—a source of water and energy.

FLAT TAIL
Leaf-tailed geckos' tails are flattened and camouflaged.

DID YOU KNOW?

Many monitors use their tail as a club to beat up attackers or prey.

TAIL AS ANCHOR
When a predator comes near, the spiny-tailed monitor uses the spines on its tail to wedge itself into a rock crevice, making it hard to drag out.

STREAMLINED TAIL
Most skinks' tails are long and streamlined.

GRIPPING TAIL
Tree-living chameleons use their tail to grip twigs.

Lizard Legs

Most lizards have four well-developed legs. Some, such as the Australian frilled-neck lizard, can run on their two large back legs for short distances. Other lizards have small limbs, or no limbs at all. These lizards usually burrow in the ground, or live in places where limbs would be of little use, such as dense grass or under leaf litter.

DID YOU KNOW?

Flap-footed lizards are snakelike, with no front legs and tiny flaplike hind legs.

Close-up of hairlike structures on a gecko's toe.

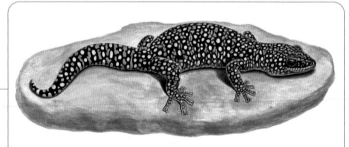

Geckos like this one climb well because their toe pads have hairlike structures (left) that cling to rough surfaces.

DISAPPEARING LEGS

Some lizards have small limbs, or sometimes none at all. This has helped them survive because they move like little snakes, wriggling through soft sand or dense bush. Lizards that spend the most time in the thickest surroundings have the smallest limbs. The bones become smaller, and in some cases, one of more sets of toe bones do not develop at all.

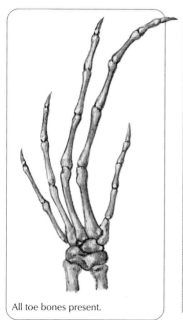

All toe bones present.

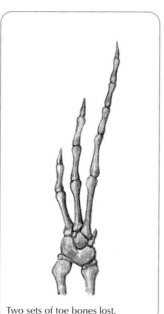

Two sets of toe bones lost.

No toes

Tongues

Most lizards use their tongues to help them eat, but they also use them to track down prey or to find a mate. They do this by "tasting" the air and ground.

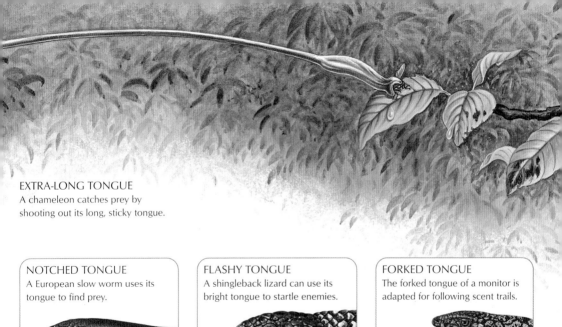

EXTRA-LONG TONGUE
A chameleon catches prey by
shooting out its long, sticky tongue.

NOTCHED TONGUE
A European slow worm uses its
tongue to find prey.

FLASHY TONGUE
A shingleback lizard can use its
bright tongue to startle enemies.

FORKED TONGUE
The forked tongue of a monitor is
adapted for following scent trails.

Watching the World

Lizards that live above the ground need good eyesight and large eyes. Those that spend their life beneath the ground have tiny eyes because they rely on senses other than sight. Lizards that are active at night need to be able to see in the dark. They have big eyes and their pupils—the transparent "holes" that let light into the eyes—are large, vertical slits. At night, these open wide to let in as much light as possible.

BEADY EYES
The bulging eyes of a chameleon move independently. This means that this lizard can see backward and forward at the same time without moving.

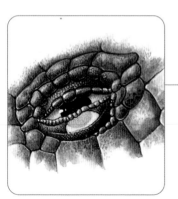 

WINDOW WITH A VIEW
Many lizards, such as skinks (left), have a small clear area on their lower eyelids (far left). This allows them to watch for predators with closed eyes.

DID YOU KNOW?

Most geckos do not have eyelids and use their tongue to clean their eyes.

Temperature Control

Like other reptiles, lizards control their body temperature with their behavior. To warm up, they move into the sun or onto a warm surface and expose as much of the body as they can to the heat. To cool down, they expose as little of the body as possible to the heat, or they move into the shade of a crevice. Many desert and tropical lizards are active at night because the night-time temperatures in these places are mild.

DID YOU KNOW?
In cold climates, lizards spend the winter in a deep burrow or crevice.

COOLING DOWN
In hot weather, a collared lizard cools down by opening its mouth to allow its saliva to evaporate.

The lizard seeks shelter during the warmest part of the day to avoid overheating.

With its body warmed, the lizard has energy for hunting, mating, and defending territory.

In the morning, the lizard basks in the sun to warm its body and get energy for a day of activity.

The lizard wakes with the sun, and emerges from its shelter.

The lizard curls up to stay as protected as possible through the night.

In the early afternoon, the lizard resumes its activities.

Late afternoon is the time to bask and digest the day's meal of insects.

As the sun begins to sink, the lizard starts to move back into its retreat.

Day and Night

Most lizards do all their activities, such as feeding and mating, during the day. Lizards that are active in the daytime must be careful not to overheat. Some lizards, such as geckos, are active at night. They emerge shortly after dark (when it is still warm) to hunt for prey at a time when other lizards are not around.

ALL-DAY IGUANA
Most desert lizards avoid the hottest part of the day. But the desert iguana goes about its business during the whole day, even when temperatures are very high.

NIGHT HUNTER
Most geckos, such as this banded gecko, are active either at night or in the near-dark hours of twilight and before sunset. They hunt for insects and spiders.

SHADES OF THE DAY

In the cool parts of the day, the skin of the rhinoceros iguana is dark to absorb the heat of the Sun. The skin is a lighter color during the hottest parts of the day to reflect heat.

Living in Dry Places

Lizards that live in dry places have to cope with high temperatures and a lack of water. Some species are active at night to escape the heat of the day. Daytime species burrow into cool sand or hide in crevices and beneath rocks during the hottest part of the day. Most desert lizards get most of the water they need from their food. All desert lizards produce droppings that are almost dry, to minimize water loss.

WATER COLLECTOR
The Australian thorny devil lives in deserts. The edges of the small scales on their legs and body form tiny channels that act like a sponge and carry water over its skin to its mouth.

DID YOU KNOW?
"Sand swimmers" are desert lizards that seem to be able to swim through loose sand.

FRINGE-TOED LIZARD
The feathery scales on this desert-living lizard's feet help to grip sand.

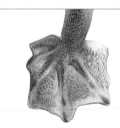

DESERT GECKO
One gecko from Africa's Namib Desert uses webbed feet to move across fine sand.

Mating Signals

Male and female marine iguanas of the Galápagos Islands are usually a grayish-black color. In the mating season, the spiny crests and front limbs of the males turn green and the sides of their body become a rusty red. These changes let the females know that the males are ready to mate.

Reproduction

Most lizards lay eggs. Some geckos
and skinks lay only one, while larger
lizards may lay forty. Other lizards,
such as the Australian blue-tongue skink, give birth to
fully formed young. Eggs are protected inside the female's
body, and the developing young are nourished by yolk, in the
same way as young that grow in eggs outside the body.

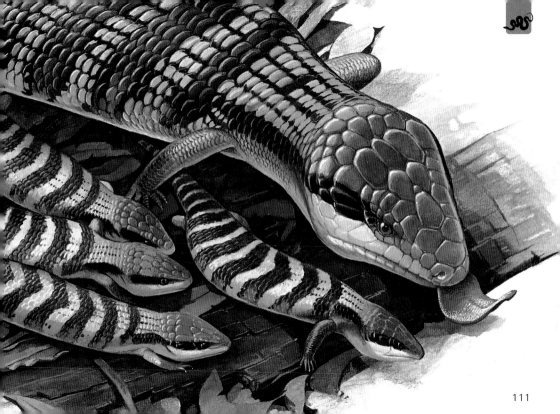

The Next Generation

A few lizards guard their eggs against predators, but most simply lay their eggs, cover them with soil and leaves, and leave them. Lizards are able to look after themselves as soon as they hatch, but there are many predators, such as birds and spiders, that try to eat the hatchlings.

> DID YOU KNOW?
> Some geckos lay sticky eggs that they often place on tree bark or leaves.

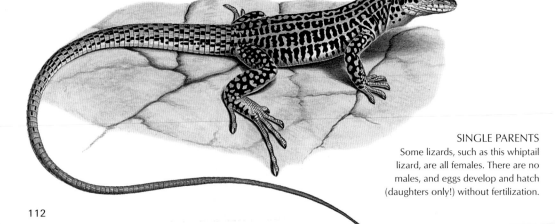

SINGLE PARENTS
Some lizards, such as this whiptail lizard, are all females. There are no males, and eggs develop and hatch (daughters only!) without fertilization.

HOUSE GUESTS

Some species of monitors keep their eggs warm and safe by burying them in termite mounds. The female has to scrape away the hard soil to help her hatchlings escape.

BOO!
The blue-tongued lizard of Australia flashes its blue tongue and hisses to frighten birds and other enemies.

Defense and Escape

Lizards have many enemies. Spiders, scorpions, other lizards, snakes, birds, and mammals all prey on them. Some lizards have special tactics to defend themselves or to escape from an attacker. Most lizards are well camouflaged and keep still until a predator passes by. Chameleons can change their color to blend in with the background. Some lizards poke out their colored tongue to startle attackers.

RUNNING ON WATER
The South American basilisk has a unique way of getting away from predators. Fringes on its toes allow it to run for short distances on its long hind legs across the surface of water.

Body Language

Most lizards live alone. They come into contact with other members of their species only for courtship and mating, and to fight over living areas. Lizards communicate using body language. They can raise their crest, extend or curl their dewlap (flap of skin on the throat), wave a front limb, thrash their tail, or change color. All of these signs mean something, from "Keep away" to "I'm ready to mate."

PUSHING UP

Collared lizards communicate with each other by bobbing their heads up and down. If another lizard enters their territory, they threaten the invader by doing "push-ups" that make them look bigger.

CALM GREEN
Male chameleons normally have dull-colored skin that blends in with the background. In the case of this species, the main color is green.

THREATENING RED
If the male wants to warn another male chameleon away from its territory, it changes its skin tone to a much brighter color, such as red.

Escaping Danger

Running fast, out of a predator's reach, is a good way to escape. Some lizards extend their neck or throat crest, hiss, or swallow air to make themselves look bigger than an attacker (or too big to swallow). Many lizards have an unusual method of escape. If grabbed by the tail, they leave it behind. The wriggling tail distracts the predator.

BLOODY ENCOUNTER

The regal horned lizard squirts a stream of its own blood up to 3 feet (1 m) to frighten an attacker.

NEW TAIL
This lizard will soon grow a new tail after dropping it to distract a predator.

TOO BIG A MOUTHFUL
Bearded dragon lizards open their yellow mouths to surprise attackers. They also expand their throats to make themselves look too big for a predator to eat.

Self-Defense

Some lizards have sharp spines that can injure a predator's mouth, or slippery scales that make them hard to grip. The armadillo girdle-tailed lizard rolls itself into a spiky ball. The Gila monster and the Mexican beaded lizard can give attackers a poisonous bite. Monitors arch their long tail when threatened and will often use it as a weapon.

SPINES FOR DEFENSE
The desert horned lizard has a row of sharp spines along its tail and sides.

SCALES AND SPIKES

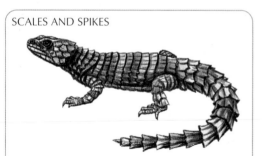

The armadillo girdle-tailed lizard of South Africa is heavily armored, with thick scales and spikes on its head and tail.

COVER-UP

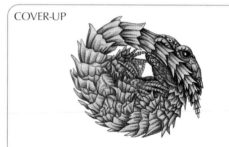

When threatened, the lizard clamps its tail in its mouth and curls itself into a ball, protecting its soft belly.

Worm Lizards

Worm lizards spend most of their time underground. They burrow through soil with their hard, strong heads. Apart from one Mexican group that has small front legs, all others have no legs at all, and look like worms or snakes.

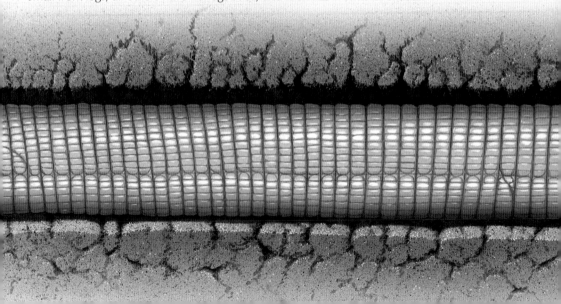

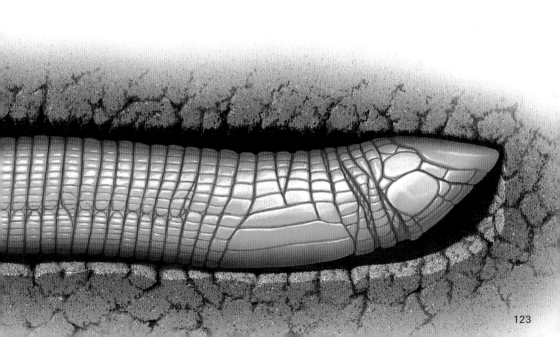

Different Heads

Worm lizards have cylinder-shaped bodies and create tunnels by burrowing with their heads. Different groups of worm lizards have different-shaped heads, depending on the method they use to burrow. Worm lizards have simple and sometimes invisible eyes. They have no openings for ears, but they can sense prey and predators through vibrations in the soil. They eat insects and other invertebrates.

DOWN BELOW
A section of the ground has been cut away to show a worm lizard lying inside its tunnel. These lizards spend most of their life underground.

DID YOU KNOW?

The Mexican worm lizard has paddle-like front legs it uses for digging.

SIDE-TO-SIDE DIGGER

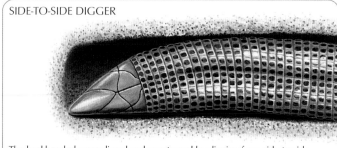

The keel-headed worm lizard makes a tunnel by digging from side to side.

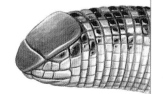

CHISEL-HEADED

These rotate the head in one direction and then in the other.

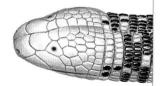

ROUND-HEADED

These push forward into the soil, and turn the head in any direction.

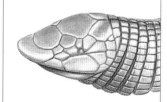

SHOVEL-HEADED

The shovel-heads push forward and then push the head up.

All about Snakes

There are almost 2,400 species of snakes.
They range in size from the length of
your arm to that of a small car. Snakes
have many different colors, patterns, and
ways of killing prey. They eat everything
from ants, eggs, snails, and slugs to animals as big as caimans
and goats. Some snakes kill by using venom, injected through
their sharp fangs; others wrap themselves so tightly around
their prey that the animal cannot breathe.

Shaped for Success

Snakes have different body shapes to suit their different environments. A ground-dwelling snake has an almost circular body. It has strong muscles to grip slippery surfaces such as sand and soil, or rough surfaces such as rocks. A tree snake's body is round at the top and flattened at the bottom and sides. This makes it easier to grip small crevices and notches on tree trunks and branches. A sea snake has a flattened body. This gives it a larger surface area with which to push against the water.

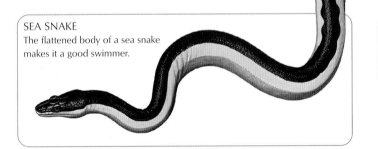

SEA SNAKE
The flattened body of a sea snake makes it a good swimmer.

DID YOU KNOW?

Vine snakes are so called because they are long and thin, and look like vines.

GROUND SNAKE
Ground dwellers have a body shape that is circular in cross-section—good for moving over most land surfaces.

TREE SNAKE
A tree snake glides through branches, thanks to a body that is shaped in cross-section almost like a loaf of bread.

The Long View

A snake is really just a long tube, which allows the animal to enter narrow crevices for food and shelter. But this tube varies greatly in size and shape from one snake group to another. The smallest snake is the 8 inch (20 cm) long thread snake; the largest is the giant anaconda, which can reach 36 feet (11 m) and weigh 440 pounds (200 kg). Snake bodies range from being shaped like a pencil to being shaped like a barrel.

BODY SHAPES
Snakes have three general body shapes: small and slender (blind snake), short and thick-bodied (viper), and shaped like a cylinder (python).

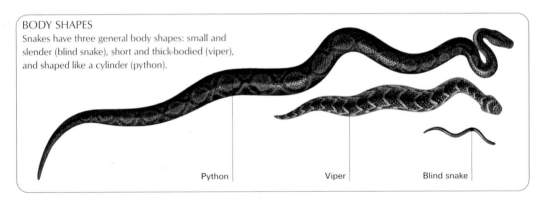

Python

Viper

Blind snake

Snake Heads

Snake heads give us clues about how and where snakes live. For example, a tree snake has a slender head just wider than its body, making it easier to move swiftly through vegetation. Most pythons, however, live on the ground and hunt large animals. Their heads are large enough to hold many teeth, which they use to hold on to struggling prey. Most snakes can open their jaws much wider than other reptiles.

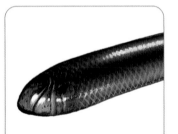

BURROWING SNAKE
A burrowing snake pushes through the soil with a solid, blunt head.

TREE SNAKE
A tree snake has a slender head to help it slip between twigs.

PYTHON
A python has a large head with powerful jaw muscles, which it uses to hold prey while it coils around the animal and squeezes it to death.

HORNED VIPER
Vipers have short, wide heads. The upper jaw is very short, with just a single large fang on either side. The wide head makes swallowing large prey easier.

Scales and Eyes

Snake skin is made up of scales. Freshwater snakes have keeled scales, which balance side-to-side movement. Snakes that burrow have smooth scales, as these make it easier to push through soil. Sea snakes have "granular" scales with a rough surface, which help them to grip fish. Eyes, too, tell us about a snake's habits. Burrowing snakes have small eyes; snakes with "cat's eye" pupils are active at night; those with large, round eyes are active in the day.

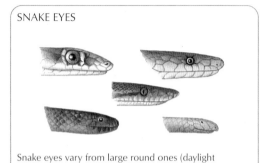

SNAKE EYES

Snake eyes vary from large round ones (daylight predators) to tiny (burrowing snakes that rarely see light).

A USEFUL SCALE

Most snakes have scales with a smooth, flat surface (far left). Some snakes have a ridge, called a keel, along the center of each scale (center). File snakes have rough, granular scales (left).

BIG EYES

Snakes active in the day need large eyes and good sight for hunting.

SMALL EYES

Night-hunters do not rely on sight to find prey and have small eyes.

EYES AT NIGHT

A snake's eyes are covered by a special clear eyelid that protects the eyes from damage. Nocturnal species often have vertical pupils, like the eyes of cats.

Shedding Skin

Snakes, like all reptiles, have a skin with an outer layer of thickened scales. As a snake grows, it sheds the dead outer layer of its scaly skin and reveals a new skin underneath. This may happen several times a year, depending on how fast the snake is growing. The old layer is not shed until a new one has completely formed underneath it. To loosen its skin, a snake rubs its nose against a hard surface and then wriggles free.

TAKE IT ALL OFF
A snake sheds its skin beginning with the head. As well as the skin of the body and head, the transparent, protective eye caps come off too.

DID YOU KNOW?
Each time a rattlesnake sheds its skin, its rattle gains a new segment.

PEELING AWAY
The old skin peels away in one piece, turning inside out as it comes off.

Snakes on the Move

Snakes have four ways to push their bodies along. A snake moves fast by pushing the side curves of its body against the surface it is traveling on (lateral undulation). In a narrow space, it presses its front coils against the sides of the space, then draws up the rest of the body (concertina movement). Heavy snakes crawl in a straight line by pushing back with sections of their belly while bringing other sections forward (rectilinear movement). Sidewinding is a way of moving on slippery surfaces, such as sand dunes.

FLYING SNAKE

The flying tree snake can glide from one tree to another.

LATERAL UNDULATION

Snakes move quickly by pushing against the ground.

CONCERTINA MOVEMENT

If they are in confined spaces, snakes move in a series of curves.

RECTILINEAR MOVEMENT

Some heavy-bodied snakes crawl in a straight line.

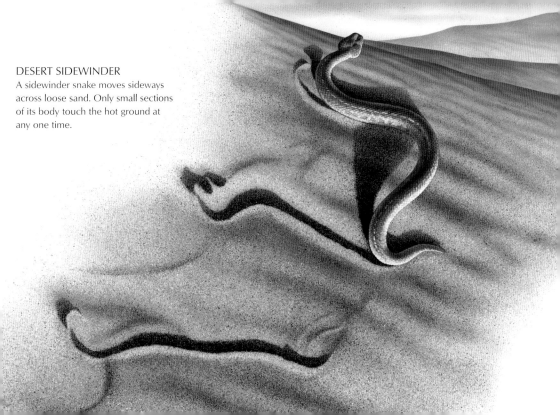

DESERT SIDEWINDER

A sidewinder snake moves sideways across loose sand. Only small sections of its body touch the hot ground at any one time.

The Inside Story

As snakes evolved from lizards, they became long and slender, and lost their limbs. Some internal organs, such as the liver and lungs, also became long and thin. Others, such as the kidneys and reproductive organs, were rearranged one behind the other in the body. In many snakes, the left lung disappeared.

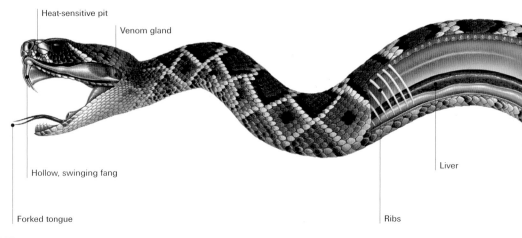

Heat-sensitive pit

Venom gland

Hollow, swinging fang

Forked tongue

Ribs

Liver

INSIDE A SNAKE
A snake, such as this rattlesnake, is like a stretched-out
cylinder. The internal organs are long and slender.

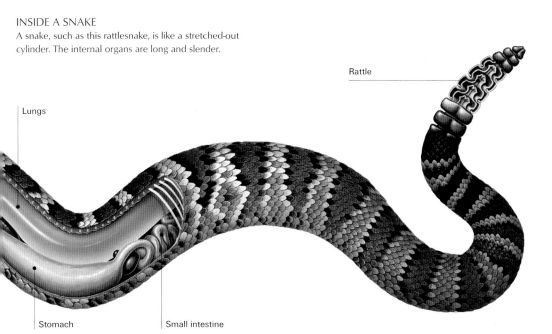

Rattle

Lungs

Stomach

Small intestine

Finding a Meal

All snakes eat animals. Some ambush, stalk, or pursue their prey. Others eat "easy" prey, such as the eggs of birds and reptiles. Many snakes, such as pythons, kill their prey by squeezing it. More than half of all snakes kill with venom, a poison injected through their fangs. Some snakes have small pits on their face that can detect heat from prey.

ON THE ATTACK
A rattlesnake's heat-sensing organs detect prey. Its fangs normally lie flat against the roof of its mouth and swing forward to inject venom.

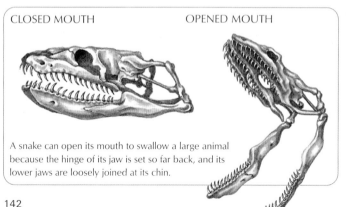

CLOSED MOUTH   OPENED MOUTH

A snake can open its mouth to swallow a large animal because the hinge of its jaw is set so far back, and its lower jaws are loosely joined at its chin.

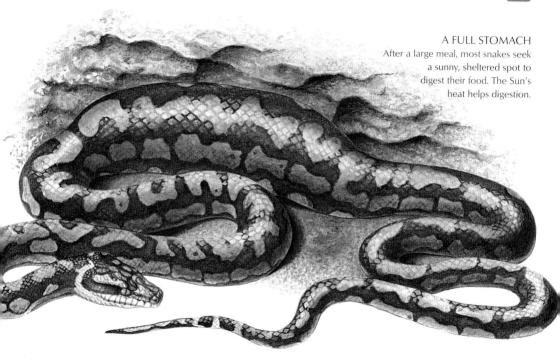

A FULL STOMACH
After a large meal, most snakes seek a sunny, sheltered spot to digest their food. The Sun's heat helps digestion.

Big Eater

Pythons are among the snakes that kill their prey by squeezing it. A python seizes its prey and wraps a series of coils around it. Whenever the prey breathes out, the python squeezes a little tighter. Eventually, the animal suffocates. A big python can swallow surprisingly large prey. It slowly "walks" its jaws forward to engulf an animal as large as a wild pig.

Sudden Death

Some snakes, such as rattlesnakes, bite and kill their prey with a poison called venom. The venom is produced in mouth glands and comes out through the snake's fangs. The prey dies within minutes, sometimes even seconds.

Types of Fangs

Venomous snakes have different kinds of fangs. Some are firmly attached to the jaw while others are hinged; some are grooved while others are hollow; some are in front of the mouth and others are at the rear. Snakes with hollow fangs inject venom into their prey, while snakes with grooved fangs let the venom ooze into the victim.

COTTONMOUTH
This venomous cottonmouth pit viper has hinged front fangs.

REAR FANGS

Venom duct

Fangs are fixed in the rear of the mouth; fangs have grooves.

FIXED FRONT FANGS

Venom duct

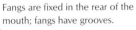

Fangs are hollow and fixed in the front of the mouth.

SWINGING FRONT FANGS

Venom duct

Fangs are hollow and swing forward to the front of the mouth.

Mother Care

In species that lay eggs, the female snake lays her eggs in a safe, warm, and slightly moist place, such as a beneath a rock. In most species, she covers the eggs and leaves them. Some snakes give birth to fully developed young. But in all cases, young snakes fend for themselves.

MOTHER'S WATCHING
Some pythons coil around their eggs to keep them warm and protect them from predators. Although she cares for the eggs, the mother leaves them when they have hatched.

ON THEIR OWN
Female snakes do not look after their young once the eggs have hatched. These young snakes will soon be on their own.

Growing Up Green

Green pythons from the rain forests of New Guinea and northern Australia do not start out green. When they hatch, they are bright yellow or brick brown in color. They become the green color of adults after one to three years.

Defense Tactics

Snakes have many enemies. They are killed and eaten by fish, lizards, other snakes, birds of prey, and mammals. They have a number of ways to defend themselves. Some camouflage or bury themselves to hide from danger. Other snakes surprise their enemies by making themselves look bigger, hissing, or lashing out with their bodies. Still others keep perfectly still, as many predators depend on movement to find their prey. There are also snakes that rely on speed for escape, moving quickly into a burrow or up a tree.

RATTLESNAKE KILLER

A king snake is not harmed by rattlesnake venom.

PLAYING DEAD

The hog-nosed snake plays dead to confuse attackers.

A FRIGHTENING SIGHT
The vine snake opens wide its brightly colored mouth to startle predators.

RATTLING DEFENSE
When disturbed, a rattlesnake will vibrate its tail to make a loud rattling sound, diverting attention to the tail and away from the striking head.

Warning Colors

Some snakes rely on bright colors to let predators know they are venomous. Red and orange, in various combinations, are the most common colors that signal danger to a predator. A few non-venomous snakes even mimic these colors.

KEEP AWAY?
Although most eyelash pit vipers of Central and South America are camouflaged in green and brown, some are this bright orange color. Perhaps it warns possible predators to beware.

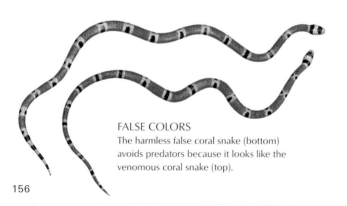

FALSE COLORS
The harmless false coral snake (bottom) avoids predators because it looks like the venomous coral snake (top).

Tuataras

The tuatara has changed little in 240 million years. It is often referred to as a "living fossil." Found only on small islands off the coast of New Zealand, tuataras are the oldest living relatives of today's snakes and lizards. The gray, olive, or reddish tuatara is not a lizard at all. The two species of tuataras are the only living members of a group of small- to medium-sized reptiles called Rhynchocephalia, or "beak-heads." Rhynchocephalians lived in most parts of the world while the dinosaurs were alive. But by 60 million years ago, they were extinct everywhere except New Zealand, which had become isolated from other landmasses.

Slowly Disappearing?

Tuataras were once found throughout the two main islands of New Zealand. Apart from birds, tuataras faced no large predators until the arrival of humans a few thousand years ago. The settlers brought with them rats and dogs, and these animals began to eat tuatara eggs and hatchlings. Today, tuataras can be found only on islands without rats.

DID YOU KNOW?

Tuataras keep growing for 35 years, and may live for more than 100 years.

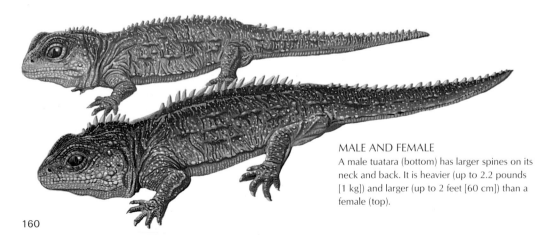

MALE AND FEMALE
A male tuatara (bottom) has larger spines on its neck and back. It is heavier (up to 2.2 pounds [1 kg]) and larger (up to 2 feet [60 cm]) than a female (top).

NIGHT BEAT

Tuataras hunt insects and other prey at night. They spend the day sleeping in their burrows or basking in the sunshine at their burrow entrances.

Where Do Reptiles Live?

Reptiles occur across most of the world's landmasses and in many oceans and seas. They are sensitive to temperature, and the number of species decreases toward the polar regions, until eventually they drop out altogether. Most species are found in tropical and subtropical areas.

TURTLES
Turtles are found on all continents except Antarctica, and in all oceans: 241 species of turtles have adapted to freshwater rivers, lakes, and ponds; 45 tortoises live on land; seven species live in the oceans.

CROCODILIANS
Crocodilians are found in all tropical, subtropical, and temperate zones: gharials in South Asia; crocodiles in Africa, South Asia, Australia, and Central and South America; and alligators in China and the Americas.

AMPHISBAENIANS

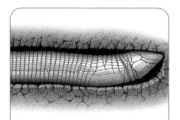

Amphisbaenians are found in tropical and subtropical regions of southern North America, South America to Patagonia, West Indies, Africa, Spain, Portugal, Arabia, and western Asia.

TUATARA

The two species of tuataras live on New Zealand islands. About 400 *Sphenodon guntheri* live on North Brother Island. More than 60,000 *S. punctatus* live on about 30 islands off the North Island.

LIZARDS

Lizards are found across a vast area of the world, from New Zealand to Norway, and from southern Canada to Tierra del Fuego. They also live on many of the islands in the world's oceans.

Reptiles around the World

The map shows the vegetation zones of the world. Which animals live in a particular area depends on the vegetation of that area. Reptiles mostly live in deserts, tropical forests, and tropical grasslands. They are not found as often in mountainous regions, on tundra, and in icy regions such as the Arctic.

- Tropical forest
- Seasonal tropical forest
- Desert
- Tropical grassland and savanna
- Mediterranean forest and scrub
- Midlatitude grassland
- Midlatitude forest
- Boreal forest
- Tundra
- Ice sheet
- Mountain vegetation

TROPICAL LIZARD
The frilled lizard is found in tropical Australia's dry woodlands, where it feeds mainly on large insects.

KINDS OF REPTILES

Turtles and Tortoises

WOOD TURTLE

The wood turtle has a shell length of about 9 inches (23 cm) and is found in deciduous forests of eastern North America, where it lives mostly on land rather than in water.

FAST FACTS

Class: Reptilia
Order: Testudinata
Family: Emydidae
Scientific name:
Clemmys insculpta
Diet: Invertebrates, plants
Location: North America

TWIST-NECKED TURTLE

The twist-necked turtle lives in freshwater streams. It is a poor swimmer. It walks along the stream bottom, staying underwater for long periods while searching for food.

FAST FACTS

Class: Reptilia
Order: Testudinata
Family: Chelidae
Scientific name:
Platemys platycephala
Diet: Insects, crayfish, tadpoles, frogs, fish
Location: South America

Turtles and Tortoises

SNAPPING TURTLE
Fish make up a large part of the American snapping turtle's diet. Much of the time is spent in the water, although these turtles also like to sunbathe in the mornings on the banks of streams and swamps.

FAST FACTS
Class: Reptilia
Order: Testudinata
Family: Chelydridae
Scientific name:
Chelydra serpentina
Diet: Fish, amphibians, birds, mammals
Location: North and Central America

BIG-HEADED TURTLE

This species is found in cool, fast-flowing mountain streams in southern China and northern and central Indo-China. Because its huge head cannot be pulled back into its shell, it is covered in armor, for protection. Its long tail is covered in armor, too.

FAST FACTS
Class: Reptilia
Order: Testudinata
Family: Platysternidae
Scientific name:
Platysternon
megacephalum
Diet: Snails, crabs, fish
Location: East Asia

Turtles and Tortoises

PAINTED TURTLE

A number of subspecies of painted turtle can be found from southern Canada to the southern United States. They live in rivers, ponds, and swamps.

FAST FACTS
Class: Reptilia
Order: Testudinata
Family: Emydidae
Scientific name:
Chrysemys picta belli
Diet: Mollusks, insects, crustaceans, fish, plants
Location: North America

EASTERN BOX TURTLE

Box turtles of eastern and southern United States and Mexico live mostly on land, and have evolved a tortoise-like appearance. Its red eyes show that this individual is a male.

FAST FACTS
Class: Reptilia
Order: Testudinata
Family: Emydidae
Scientific name:
Terrapene carolina carolina
Diet: Berries, fungi, mollusks, worms, insects
Location: North America

Turtles and Tortoises

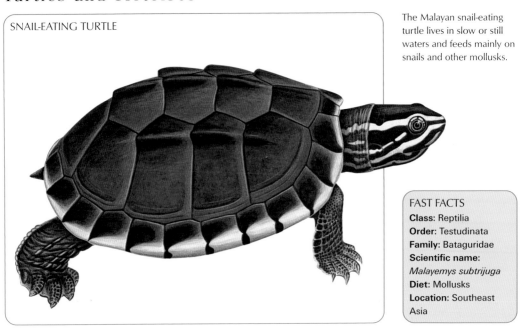

SNAIL-EATING TURTLE

The Malayan snail-eating turtle lives in slow or still waters and feeds mainly on snails and other mollusks.

FAST FACTS
Class: Reptilia
Order: Testudinata
Family: Bataguridae
Scientific name:
Malayemys subtrijuga
Diet: Mollusks
Location: Southeast Asia

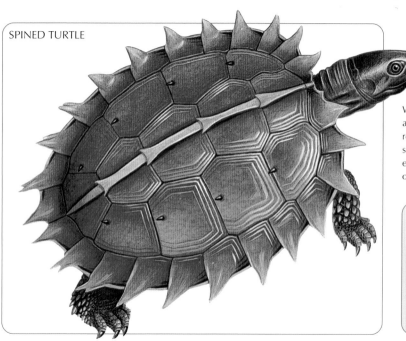

SPINED TURTLE

When young, this turtle has a circular shell edged with regular spines. In adults the spines are less obvious, except on the rear edges of the shell.

FAST FACTS

Class: Reptilia
Order: Testudinata
Family: Bataguridae
Scientific name:
Heosemys spinosa
Diet: Plants
Location: Southeast Asia

Turtles and Tortoises

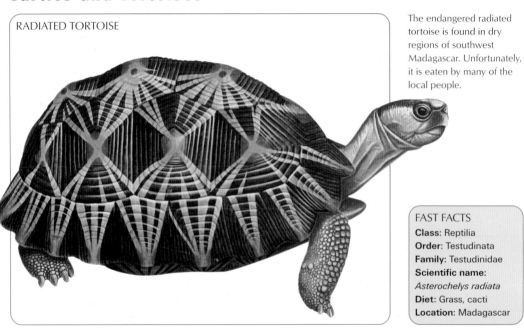

RADIATED TORTOISE

The endangered radiated tortoise is found in dry regions of southwest Madagascar. Unfortunately, it is eaten by many of the local people.

FAST FACTS
Class: Reptilia
Order: Testudinata
Family: Testudinidae
Scientific name:
Asterochelys radiata
Diet: Grass, cacti
Location: Madagascar

GALÁPAGOS TORTOISE

These tortoises live on seven islands of the Galápagos archipelago, where they move between the grassy lowlands (in the cooler months) and the volcanic highlands (in the hot, dry season).

FAST FACTS

Class: Reptilia
Order: Testudinata
Family: Testudinidae
Scientific name:
Chelonoidis elephantopus
Diet: Grass, cacti
Location: Galápagos Islands

Turtles and Tortoises

EASTERN SPINY SOFTSHELL TURTLE

These turtles have light and flexible shells and a snorkel-like snout. They are fast swimmers in open water, and can stay underwater for longer than most aquatic turtles.

FAST FACTS

Class: Reptilia
Order: Testudinata
Family: Trionychidae
Scientific name:
Apalone spinifera
Diet: Mollusks, insects, crustaceans, fish, frogs
Location: North America

SOUTHERN LOGGERHEAD MUSK TURTLE

This musk turtle spends most of its day walking on the bottom of streams and lakes looking for food. When disturbed, it releases a strong musky smell.

FAST FACTS

Class: Reptilia
Order: Testudinata
Family: Kinosternidae
Scientific name:
Sternotherus minor minor
Diet: Insects, spiders, frogs, fish, plants
Location: USA

Turtles and Tortoises

LEATHERBACK TURTLE
The leatherback is the largest of all turtles—individuals with shells of more than 5 feet (1.5 m) are not uncommon. Unlike other sea turtles, whose shells are covered by horny plates, the shell of this species is covered only by a leathery skin.

FAST FACTS
Class: Reptilia
Order: Testudinata
Family: Dermochelyidae
Scientific name: *Dermochelys coriacea*
Diet: Mainly jellyfish
Location: Tropical to temperate seas

HAWKSBILL TURTLE

The hawksbill's beautiful carapace was the source of commercial "tortoise shell," used in the manufacture of eyeglasses frames, and combs. It is classified as an endangered species.

FAST FACTS

Class: Reptilia
Order: Testudinata
Family: Cheloniidae
Scientific name:
Eretmochelys imbricata
Diet: Fish, jellyfish, sponges, crabs, clams, mussels, sea urchins
Location: Tropical seas

Crocodilians

CUVIER'S DWARF CAIMAN

BLACK CAIMAN

FAST FACTS
Class: Reptilia
Order: Crocodilia
Family: Alligatoridae
Scientific name:
Paleosuchus
palpebrosus
Diet: Fish, invertebrates
Location: South
America

The smallest crocodilian, this species grows to about 5 feet (1.5 m) for males and 4 feet (1.2 m) for females. It lives in forests, and spends much of its time away from water.

FAST FACTS
Class: Reptilia
Order: Crocodilia
Family: Alligatoridae
Scientific name:
Melanosuchus niger
Diet: Fish, mammals,
reptiles
Location: South
America

The black caiman lives in the Amazon basin and nearby coastal rivers. Intensive hunting for its skin in the 1950s and 1960s quickly reduced the species to critically low numbers.

COMMON CAIMAN

An extremely adaptable crocodilian, this species occurs in virtually all open habitats such as savannas, swamps, large rivers, and lakes. It also invades habitats created by humans, such as cattle ponds and dams.

FAST FACTS

Class: Reptilia
Order: Crocodilia
Family: Alligatoridae
Scientific name:
Caiman crocodilus
Diet: Water snails, fish
Location: South and Central America

Crocodilians

NILE CROCODILE

The Nile crocodile is the biggest and strongest freshwater predator in Africa. It kills big animals, such as buffaloes, by dragging them into the water and drowning them.

FAST FACTS
Class: Reptilia
Order: Crocodilia
Family: Crocodylidae
Scientific name:
Crocodylus niloticus
Diet: Fish, birds, mammals
Location: Africa

SIAMESE CROCODILE

This 13 foot (4 m) crocodile lives in freshwater lakes, rivers, and marshes. Little is known about it, and it is now thought to be extinct in the wild.

FAST FACTS
Class: Reptilia
Order: Crocodilia
Family: Crocodylidae
Scientific name:
Crocodylus siamensis
Diet: Probably fish, snakes, frogs, insects
Location: Southeast Asia

Crocodilians

CUBAN CROCODILE

The Cuban crocodile inhabits pools and channels in freshwater swamps, and grows to about 11½ feet (3.5 m) in length. Very little is known of its habits.

FAST FACTS
Class: Reptilia
Order: Crocodilia
Family: Crocodylidae
Scientific name:
Crocodylus rhombifer
Diet: Fish, turtles, mammals
Location: Cuba

ORINOCO CROCODILE

This large species grows to 20 feet (6 m) or more. It is found only in the freshwater reaches of the Orinoco River in Colombia and Venezuela.

FAST FACTS
Class: Reptilia
Order: Crocodilia
Family: Crocodylidae
Scientific name:
Crocodylus intermedius
Diet: Fish, mammals, amphibians, reptiles
Location: South America

Crocodilians

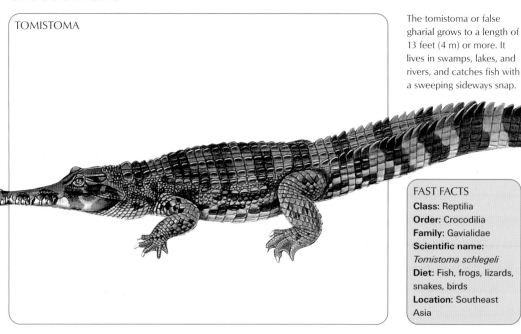

TOMISTOMA

The tomistoma or false gharial grows to a length of 13 feet (4 m) or more. It lives in swamps, lakes, and rivers, and catches fish with a sweeping sideways snap.

FAST FACTS

Class: Reptilia
Order: Crocodilia
Family: Gavialidae
Scientific name:
Tomistoma schlegeli
Diet: Fish, frogs, lizards, snakes, birds
Location: Southeast Asia

GHARIAL

The gharial is easily identified by its long, slender snout, the male's having a knob at the tip. It spends more time in water than other crocodilians.

FAST FACTS

Class: Reptilia
Order: Crocodilia
Family: Gavialidae
Scientific name:
Gavialis gangeticus
Diet: Fish
Location: Indian subcontinent

Lizards

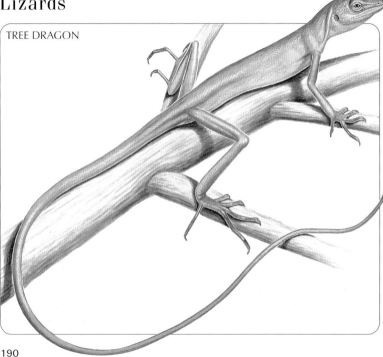

TREE DRAGON

When still, the tree dragon's thin, sticklike body and limbs make it almost invisible in trees. Its green coloring also helps to camouflage it among trees with thin, green leaves.

FAST FACTS

Class: Reptilia
Order: Squamata
Family: Agamidae
Scientific name:
Diporiphora superba
Diet: Insects, spiders
Location: Australia

FRILLED LIZARD

This tree-dwelling lizard is active during the day in dry grasslands. When escaping, it runs on two legs. If threatened, it spreads its huge frilled collar to appear much larger than it is.

Lizards

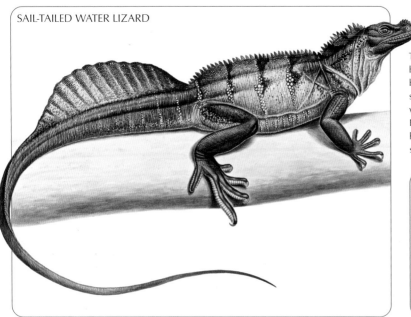

SAIL-TAILED WATER LIZARD

This semi-aquatic lizard basks on rocks and branches at the edge of streams, retreating to the water when in danger. Helped by fringes on its hind toes, it can run on the surface of the water.

FAST FACTS
Class: Reptilia
Order: Squamata
Family: Agamidae
Scientific name:
Hydrosaurus ambionensis
Diet: Invertebrates
Location: Indonesia, New Guinea

MALAGASY CHAMELEON

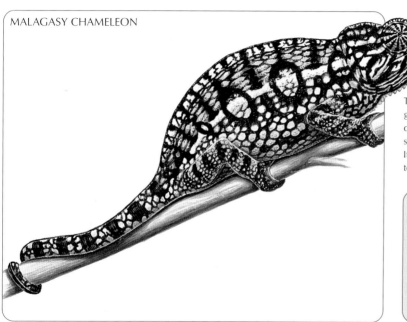

This species is usually dull green in color. When disturbed, it takes on the striking pattern shown here. It uses its long, sticky tongue to catch small prey.

Lizards

FIJIAN CRESTED IGUANA

This species probably evolved from mainland South American iguanas that accidentally drifted across the Pacific Ocean on floating vegetation.

FAST FACTS
Class: Reptilia
Order: Squamata
Family: Iguanidae
Scientific name:
Brachylophus vitiensis
Diet: Plants, insects
Location: Fiji

MARINE IGUANA

Found throughout the Galápagos Islands, the marine iguana is the only lizard to venture into the sea. Larger males can dive to depths of 40 feet (12 m) or more.

FAST FACTS
Class: Reptilia
Order: Squamata
Family: Iguanidae
Scientific name:
Amblyrhynchus cristatus
Diet: Marine algae, seaweed
Location: Galápagos Islands

CUBAN BROWN ANOLE

Climbing pads on its front toes make this anole an expert climber. The male displays its colorful dewlap to advertise ownership of a territory or to attract a mate. The female digs a nest in the ground where she lays her eggs.

FAST FACTS

Class: Reptilia
Order: Squamata
Family: Iguanidae
Scientific name: *Anolis sagrei sagrei*
Diet: Insects, fruits
Location: Cuba

Lizards

SHORT-HORNED LIZARD

The short-horned lizard is about the same size as a human hand. Like other horned lizards, it lives in deserts, but at higher altitudes. It gives birth to live young.

FAST FACTS

Class: Reptilia
Order: Squamata
Family: Phyrnosomatidae
Scientific name: *Phrynosoma douglassi*
Diet: Insects, spiders
Location: North America

DESERT HORNED LIZARD

This species is found in the western American deserts. It spends the first few hours of the day basking in the sun, after which it forages for food. In the evening, to avoid the cool night air, it digs itself into the sand.

FAST FACTS

Class: Reptilia
Order: Squamata
Family: Phyrnosomatidae
Scientific name: *Phrynosoma platyrhinos*
Diet: Insects, spiders
Location: North America

Lizards

FLAP-FOOTED LIZARD

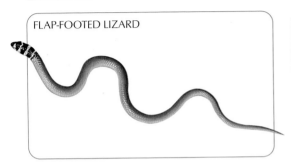

COLLARED LIZARD

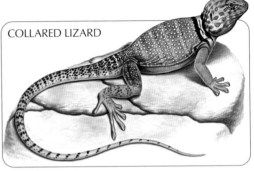

FAST FACTS
Class: Reptilia
Order: Squamata
Family: Pygopodiae
Scientific name: *Delma tincta*
Diet: Lizards, snakes
Location: Australia

With its extremely long body, tiny hind legs, and no front legs, this lizard looks remarkably like a snake. It can use the strong muscles in its tail to lift its entire body off the ground.

FAST FACTS
Class: Reptilia
Order: Squamata
Family: Crotaphytidae
Scientific name: *Crotaphytus collaris*
Diet: Small lizards, snakes, mammals
Location: North America

The collared lizard lives among piles of rock but prefers limestone ledges that provide open spaces to run across and crevices to hide in. It often runs on only its back legs.

SHELTOPUSIK

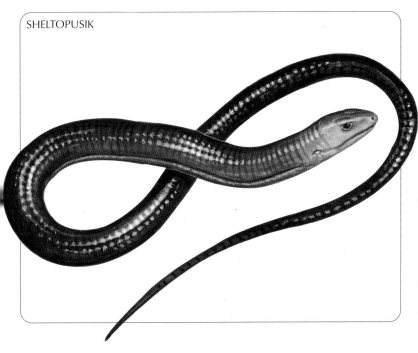

Reaching a length of up to 4½ feet (1.4 m), this is the largest of the glass lizards. Less secretive than other species, it can often be seen basking on the branches of low bushes.

FAST FACTS

Class: Reptilia
Order: Squamata
Family: Anguidae
Scientific name:
Pseudopus apodus
Diet: Small mammals, snails, insects, reptiles
Location: Europe, Asia

Lizards

VELVET GECKO

BLUE-TAILED DAY GECKO

FAST FACTS
Class: Reptilia
Order: Squamata
Family: Diplodactylidae
Scientific name:
Oedura tryoni
Diet: Insects, spiders
Location: Australia

The southern spotted velvet gecko is found on granite outcrops on Australia's east coast. Velvet geckos have tiny, even scales that give their skin a velvety texture.

FAST FACTS
Class: Reptilia
Order: Squamata
Family: Gekkonidae
Scientific name:
Phelsuma cepediana
Diet: Insects, spiders, fruits, nectar, pollen
Location: Réunion, Mauritius

Being active during daytime and a tree dweller, this gecko has round pupils and greatly reduced claws. It relies solely on its toe pads when climbing.

RING-TAILED GECKO

This species usually forages for food on the ground or on rocks or cliff faces, but it is an excellent climber and can sometimes be seen perched on low branches or tree trunks.

FAST FACTS

Class: Reptilia
Order: Squamata
Family: Gekkonidae
Scientific name:
Cyrtodactylus louisiadensis
Diet: Insects, lizards
Location: Australia

Lizards

PERENTIE

Australia's largest monitor, the perentie, grows to 8 feet (2½ m) in length. Male perenties compete for females, rising up on their hind legs and "wrestling." The winner is the one who pushes his opponent over.

FAST FACTS

Class: Reptilia
Order: Squamata
Family: Varanidae
Scientific name:
Varanus giganteus
Diet: Small mammals, birds, lizards, carrion
Location: Australia

ARMADILLO GIRDLE-TAILED LIZARD

This heavily armored lizard of South Africa's rocky, mountainous areas rolls itself into a ball when threatened. A rock dweller, it is active during the day.

FAST FACTS

Class: Reptilia
Order: Squamata
Family: Cordylidae
Scientific name:
Cordylus cataphractus
Diet: Insects
Location: Africa

Lizards

FLAT LIZARD

FAST FACTS

Class: Reptilia
Order: Squamata
Family: Cordylidae
Scientific name:
Platysaurus guttatus
Diet: Insects
Location: Africa

These lizards have an amazingly flat head and body that allow them to squeeze into the narrowest of rock crevices. Males become vibrantly colored during the breeding season.

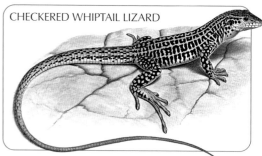

CHECKERED WHIPTAIL LIZARD

FAST FACTS

Class: Reptilia
Order: Squamata
Family: Teiidae
Scientific name:
Cnemidophorus tesselatus
Diet: Insects, termites
Location: North America

This is an all-female species, able to produce fertile eggs without mating with males. The checkered whiptail is an active forager, at times moving almost constantly in search of prey.

COMMON JUNGLE RUNNER

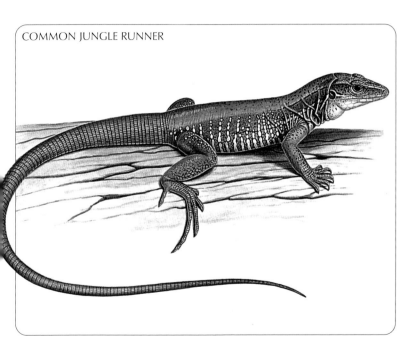

Found along river banks or in forest clearings, the common jungle runner hunts for a wide variety of prey, from beetles and caterpillars to small birds and other reptiles.

FAST FACTS

Class: Reptilia
Order: Squamata
Family: Teiidae
Scientific name:
Ameiva ameiva
Diet: Insects, spiders, birds, mammals, reptiles, leaves, fruits
Location: Latin America

Lizards

ITALIAN WALL LIZARD

Wall lizards have a long body with a pointed head, well-developed limbs, and a long, tapering tail. They can often be seen climbing on trees or rocks, or basking on old stone walls.

FAST FACTS

Class: Reptilia
Order: Squamata
Family: Lacertidae
Scientific name:
Podarcis sicula
Diet: Insects
Location:
Mediterranean

GRANITE NIGHT LIZARD

This nocturnal lizard of the Californian deserts lives in rock cracks and crevices. Like many lizards, its tail will break off if pulled. A new tail will grow in its place but it will be all one color.

FAST FACTS
Class: Reptilia
Order: Squamata
Family: Xantusiidae
Scientific name:
Xantusia henshawi
Diet: Insects
Location: USA

Lizards

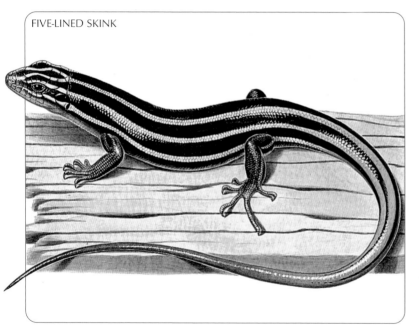

FIVE-LINED SKINK

The five-lined skink prefers damp, wooded areas, decaying leaf litter, rotting stumps, and logs, but can also be seen in gardens. The bright blue tail of juveniles disappears in adults and the body becomes brown.

FAST FACTS

Class: Reptilia
Order: Squamata
Family: Scincidae
Scientific name: *Eumeces fasciatus*
Diet: Insects, spiders, crustaceans, lizards, earthworms, small mice
Location: North America

PINK-TONGUED SKINK

This species shelters under loose tree bark or rock shelves, or in cracks and crevices. It usually forages for its prey on the ground but also climbs well through low vegetation.

FAST FACTS

Class: Reptilia
Order: Squamata
Family: Scincidae
Scientific name:
Cyclodomorphus gerrardii
Diet: Mainly slugs and snails, some insects
Location: Australia

Snakes

BLOTCHED PIPE SNAKE

The blotched pipe snake burrows through damp soil and mud looking for prey. It raises its brightly colored tail to mimic a cobra's head and hood.

FAST FACTS
Class: Reptilia
Order: Squamata
Family: Aniliidae
Scientific name:
Cylindrophus maculatus
Diet: Small mammals, reptiles
Location: Sri Lanka

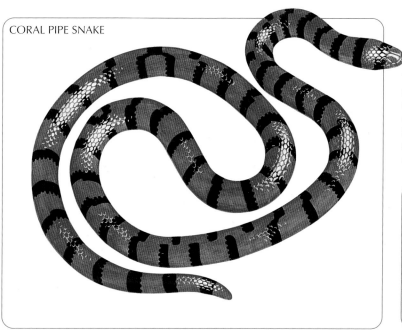

CORAL PIPE SNAKE

The colors and markings of this non-venomous species mimic those of the venomous coral snake. It lives in swamps and marshy areas in the forests of the Amazon basin.

FAST FACTS
Class: Reptilia
Order: Squamata
Family: Aniliidae
Scientific name: *Anilius scytale*
Diet: Small mammals, reptiles
Location: South America

Snakes

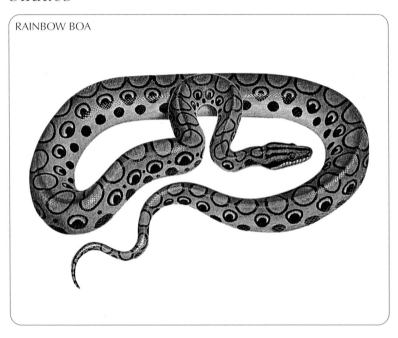

RAINBOW BOA

This nocturnal boa spends part of its time in trees, but feeds on the ground. It is often found near village outskirts where there is a steady supply of rodents and other food.

FAST FACTS

Class: Reptilia
Order: Squamata
Family: Boidae
Scientific name:
Epicrates cenchria cenchria
Diet: Small mammals, lizards, birds
Location: Central and South America

KENYAN SAND BOA

This burrowing snake is rarely seen above ground during the daytime. It digs its way through sand or loose soil with its blunt, shovel-shaped snout.

> **FAST FACTS**
> **Class:** Reptilia
> **Order:** Squamata
> **Family:** Boidae
> **Scientific name:** *Eryx colubrinus*
> **Diet:** Rodents, birds, lizards
> **Location:** Africa

Snakes

SPOTTED HARLEQUIN SNAKE

While the venom of the spotted harlequin snake is toxic to humans, few bites have been recorded. It is often found in old termite mounds, under stones, or in other hiding places.

FAST FACTS
Class: Reptilia
Order: Squamata
Family: Colubridae
Scientific name:
Homoroselaps lacteus
Diet: Reptiles
Location: Africa

SLUG-EATING SNAKE

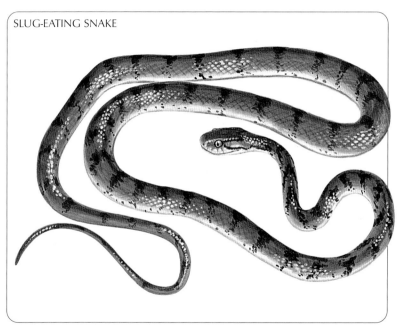

To get at its main prey of snails, this snake first inserts its elongated lower jaw into a snail's shell. The long front teeth hook into the snail's body, which the snake drags out with twisting movements.

FAST FACTS
Class: Reptilia
Order: Squamata
Family: Colubridae
Scientific name:
Pareas formosensis
Diet: Snails, slugs
Location: Asia

Snakes

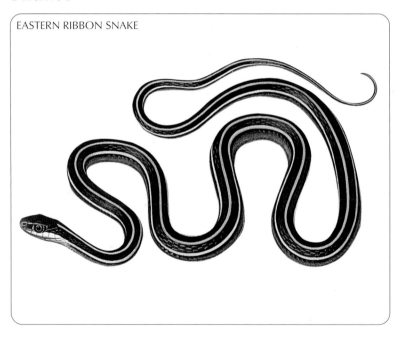

EASTERN RIBBON SNAKE

Semi-aquatic ribbon snakes are rarely found far from water. They like to bask in bushes on the shoreline, but if startled will take to the water, gliding swiftly across the surface.

FAST FACTS

Class: Reptilia
Order: Squamata
Family: Colubridae
Scientific name:
Thamnophis sauritus sauritus
Diet: Fish, amphibians, earthworms
Location: North America

WESTERN GARTER SNAKE

Garter snakes are semi-aquatic and always found near water. They live on the margins of lakes, streams, ponds, marshes, swamps, drainage ditches, and irrigation canals.

FAST FACTS

Class: Reptilia
Order: Squamata
Family: Colubridae
Scientific name:
Thamnophis couchi
Diet: Fish, amphibians, earthworms
Location: North America

Snakes

FAST FACTS
Class: Reptilia
Order: Squamata
Family: Colubridae
Scientific name: *Elaphe mandarina*
Diet: Mammals, frogs, lizards, birds, eggs
Location: China

MANDARIN RATSNAKE
This brilliantly colored snake comes from high-altitude regions of China. Ratsnakes are non-venomous constrictors that spend much of their time in burrows looking for food.

FAST FACTS
Class: Reptilia
Order: Squamata
Family: Colubridae
Scientific name: *Imantodes cenchoa*
Diet: Lizards, frogs
Location: Central and South America

BLUNT-HEADED TREE SNAKE
This species has a very long and slender body. It forages among tree branches at night, and subdues its prey with venom using fangs at the back of its mouth.

RED-SIDED GARTER SNAKE

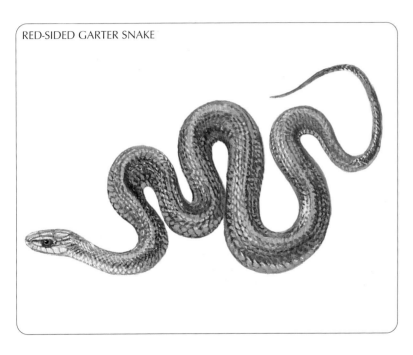

This subspecies of the common garter snake lives in Canada, where it hibernates in large groups in deep crevices. In spring, thousands of these snakes emerge at the same time to bask in the sun and breed.

FAST FACTS

Class: Reptilia
Order: Squamata
Family: Colubridae
Scientific name:
Thamnophis sirtalis parietalis
Diet: Earthworms, slugs, frogs, fish
Location: Canada

Snakes

ARIZONA CORAL SNAKE

These brightly colored snakes have very potent venom. Their startling bands of red, black, and yellow warn predators to stay away.

FAST FACTS
Class: Reptilia
Order: Squamata
Family: Elapidae
Scientific name:
Micruroides
euryxanthus
euryxanthus
Diet: Lizards, snakes
Location: USA

GABOON ADDER

The beautiful markings of this African adder give it superb camouflage. To kill its prey, it injects venom with one quick strike and then waits. Even if the animal runs away to die, the viper can follow its scent trail.

FAST FACTS
Class: Reptilia
Order: Squamata
Family: Viperidae
Scientific name: *Bitis gabonica*
Diet: Frogs, lizards, birds, small mammals
Location: Africa

ALL ABOUT
AMPHIBIANS

Salamanders and Newts

Salamanders and newts all have long tails and most have four legs. They look a bit like lizards, but their lack of scales is one factor that sets them apart from that group. Most species are secretive. They live on land in leaf litter or rotting logs, underground, inside certain plants, or underwater. Salamanders and newts belong to the order Caudata, and most of them are found in the Northern Hemisphere.

ALPINE NEWT
Newts live in water for at least part of the time. This male alpine newt from Europe has developed finlike extensions on its tail and back.

TYPICAL SALAMANDER
The two-lined salamander of North America shows the typical salamander form: a long, narrow body, long tail, and four fairly short limbs.

Salamanders: Inside and Outside

Salamanders evolved to live on land, with four legs and a tail. Some species have returned to live permanently in the water and have small limbs and a long eel-like tail; these are called sirens. Many species of salamander are brightly colored to warn their major predators—birds—that they taste nasty.

PACIFIC GIANT

The Pacific giant salamander grows to about 14 inches (36 cm) in length. It is found in western North Americia.

FIRE SALAMANDER

The fire salamander is found across a wide area of Europe. Like most salamanders, it has a smooth, moist, and flexible skin.

FIRE SALAMANDER SKELETON

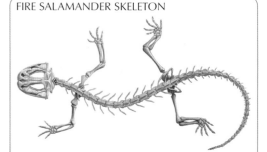

The fire salamander's skeleton has a spinal column that is rigid to support the head, but with enough flexibility to allow the body to move sideways.

Salamanders versus Newts

The word "salamander" refers to all members of the order Caudata, whereas "newt" applies to a number of species within this order. In general, salamanders have moist, slippery skin and are mostly land dwellers. Newts differ from other salamanders by living most of their lives in water. They develop fins along their tails to help them swim.

FOREST DWELLER
The completely terrestrial yellow-eyed salamander, of the Pacific coast of North America, lives under logs and rocks on the forest floor.

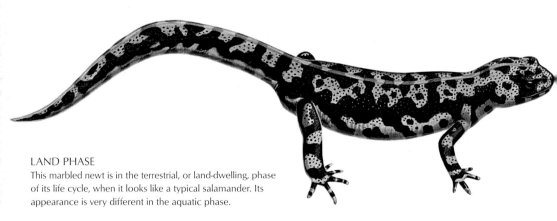

LAND PHASE
This marbled newt is in the terrestrial, or land-dwelling, phase of its life cycle, when it looks like a typical salamander. Its appearance is very different in the aquatic phase.

Salamander Life Cycles

There is no one life cycle that applies to all salamanders. Some species live, mate, and lay eggs in water, while others are totally terrestrial. The most common life cycle is called amphibious, with adults spending most of their time on land but migrating to water to breed. The larvae have gills and fins. They undergo metamorphosis to become juveniles, losing the gills and fins, and leave the water to live on land.

DID YOU KNOW?

As it grows, a salamander sheds its skin, usually eating it as it comes off.

SKIPPING A STAGE

This arboreal salamander of North America lays eggs that hatch directly into small salamanders, skipping the larval stage of amphibious species.

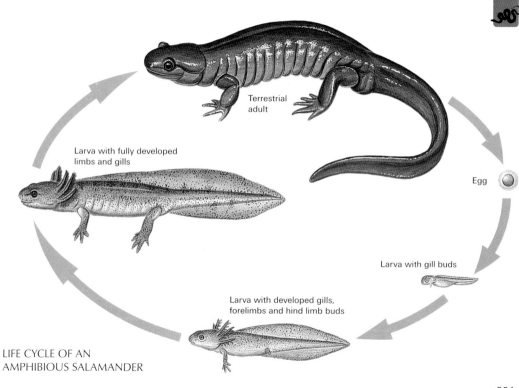

Terrestrial adult

Egg

Larva with fully developed limbs and gills

Larva with gill buds

Larva with developed gills, forelimbs and hind limb buds

LIFE CYCLE OF AN AMPHIBIOUS SALAMANDER

Mating

Salamanders and newts have intricate courtship rituals, including dances. Courtship in *Euproctus* newts involves a sort of embrace. In some species, males fertilize the eggs outside the female's body. In other salamanders, fertilization takes place inside the female. On land, eggs can be laid in several different places as long as there is enough humidity and protection. In water, they are attached to rocks or submerged tree roots. In several species, females give birth to adult-like young.

THE NEXT GENERATION
Instead of laying eggs, the female fire salamander gives birth either to well-developed larvae or young that almost perfectly resemble the adults.

DID YOU KNOW?

In some species, the male stimulates the female by rubbing a secretion on her.

UNDER GUARD

The four-toed salamander lays its eggs under logs or in moss near creeks. The female guards them until they hatch; the larvae enter the water to finish development.

COURTSHIP CONSEQUENCES

During courtship, males of species that fertilize their eggs internally deposit packets of sperm, called spermatophores, below the females, which pick them up with their cloacal lips.

Forever Young

Salamander larvae swim with fins and breathe through gills. After a period of time, in most species the larvae undergo metamorphosis. They lose the fins and gills and develop adult characteristics. But in some species larvae do not go through metamorphosis. They become mature and are able to reproduce while still looking like larvae. This condition is called neoteny. In some species, neoteny is permanent; in others, it lasts until something in the environment changes.

DID YOU KNOW?

Although it is popular as a pet, the axolotl is endangered in the wild.

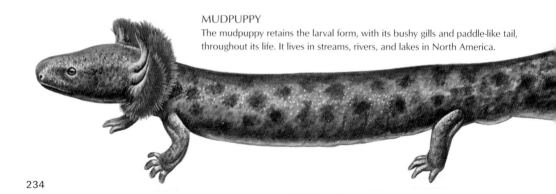

MUDPUPPY
The mudpuppy retains the larval form, with its bushy gills and paddle-like tail, throughout its life. It lives in streams, rivers, and lakes in North America.

AXOLOTL
The axolotl is a familiar aquarium pet, but in the wild, it lives only in two small lakes near Mexico City.

Breathing without Lungs

Many salamanders do not have lungs. They breathe through their skin and the lining of their mouth. Because their skin must remain moist to absorb oxygen, these animals spend much of their time hidden away in damp places. They shelter in caves, crevices in rocks, spaces between roots and stones, or under logs. They come out only when it is humid and the temperature is mild, usually on rainy nights.

SLIMY SALAMANDER
Lungless salamanders make their homes in damp habitats. This slimy salamander lives in forests under rocks and logs, and in rotten tree stumps.

RED SALAMANDER

The red salamander is a lungless
species from central and eastern
North America, where it is found near
brooks and springs.

RED-BACK SALAMANDER

Most lungless species live in the Americas, from
southern Canada south to Bolivia and Brazil. The
red-back is from North America.

Staying Alive

Salamanders feed mainly on small invertebrates such as insects, spiders, crustaceans, mollusks, and worms. While looking for food, they in turn are preyed upon by other animals. These include other amphibians, turtles, snakes, birds, mammals, and even large beetles. Some salamanders defend themselves by secreting toxic or sticky substances.

RISKY LIVING
Many animals feed on salamanders. Here, a red-back salamander is being eaten by a ring-neck snake.

DID YOU KNOW?
Most salamanders are silent, but a few species can produce a weak squeak.

TASTY MEAL
An earthworm is on the menu for this spotted salamander.

Warning Colors

Many species of salamanders are brightly colored to warn predators that they are distasteful or even poisonous. Some newts assume a rigid posture that displays their brightly colored undersides. One posture involves arching the body with the tail held straight up (or sometimes rolled up) to reveal the brightly colored underside of the tail and body.

POISON IN RESERVE
The fire salamander backs up its warning colors with a potent defense: it can squirt poison at attackers.

KEEP AWAY!
The tiger salamander is one of the most strikingly colored of all salamanders. Its bright yellow-and-black markings warn potential predators to keep their distance.

Caecilians

Caecilians are long, wormlike burrowing amphibians. They are found only in the tropical and subtropical regions of the world. Although their name (pronounced "see-sil-e-an") means "blind," most caecilians have small eyes. They rarely emerge from their burrows, so they are very difficult to find and observe. Caecilians are so little known, in fact, that most of them have no common name.

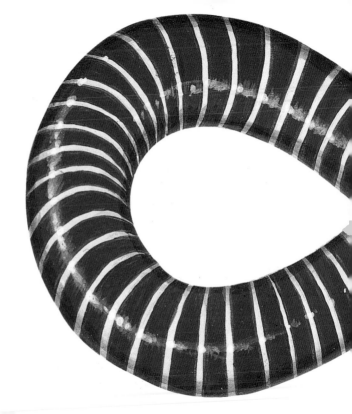

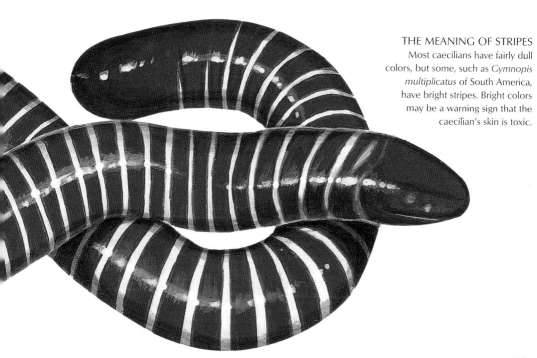

THE MEANING OF STRIPES
Most caecilians have fairly dull colors, but some, such as *Gymnopis multiplicatus* of South America, have bright stripes. Bright colors may be a warning sign that the caecilian's skin is toxic.

Life Underground

Caecilians can move snakelike across land when forced to do so, but normally they live underground. They move through existing tunnels or create new ones by pushing their head through moist soil or loose mud. Some species live wholly on land (terrestrial); others spend most of their time in water (aquatic); still others are semi-aquatic. Even the most aquatic species can burrow into the soft mud and gravel on the bottoms and edges of the streams and rivers where they live.

MEDIUM SIZE
Caecilians vary in length from 3 inches (7 cm) to nearly 5 feet (1.5 m). *Dermophis mexicanus* of Mexico and Central America is a terrestrial species that grows to more than 2 feet (60 cm) in length.

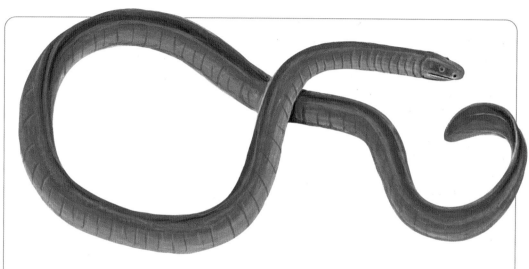

SWIMMING CAECILIAN
Aquatic caecilians such as *Typhlonectes natans* of South America are flattened from side to side and have a fin running the length of their back to make swimming easier.

Built for Burrowing

Caecilians are well adapted to burrowing. Their skull is powerfully built with a pointed snout and underslung or recessed mouth—features that allow their head to be used as a ram. Two sets of powerful muscles in the head keep their jaws firmly closed while burrowing. Their eyes are reduced in size and importance, as there is no light in their underground world. Caecilians use tentacles on their head to sense the environment.

BETTER BURROWERS
While typical vertebrates have one set of jaw-closing muscles, caecilians have two. The more efficient burrowers among caecilians make more use of the second set of jaw muscles, reflected by the increased muscle size shown in the illustrations.

VISION NOT IMPORTANT
The eyes of this species are tiny black dots, indicating the unimportance of vision for these amphibians. In some caecilians, the eyes are hidden beneath the bones of the skull.

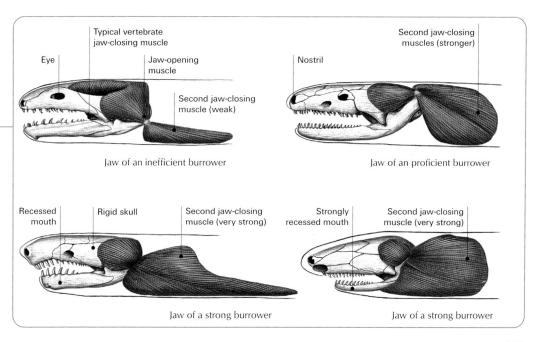

Jaw of an inefficient burrower

Jaw of a proficient burrower

Jaw of a strong burrower

Jaw of a strong burrower

Young Caecilians

Fertilization takes places inside the female, unlike most other amphibians. Some species lay eggs that hatch into water-dwelling larvae, which later undergo metamorphosis and become adults. Others lay eggs that hatch directly into land-dwelling juveniles without passing through a larval stage. However, most caecilians give birth to live young, and there is no larval stage.

AT THE NEST
This sticky caecilian of Southeast Asia is guarding her eggs, which she has laid in an underground chamber. She will abandon her young at hatching.

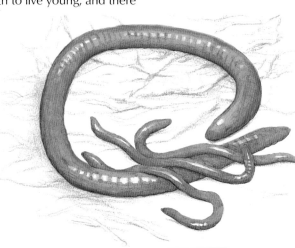

NEW MOTHER
Caecilians like this one give birth to small but fully formed versions of themselves.

DID YOU KNOW?

Female caecilians of egg-laying species stay with their eggs until they hatch.

FROGS AND TOADS

From Egg to Adult

Most of the world's frogs grow from egg to adult in the same way. Eggs are laid in water and hatch into free-living tadpoles, which have gills and a tail and feed on algae. The tadpoles undergo metamorphosis, in which the tail shrinks, and lungs and legs develop. The young frogs leave the water and reach maturity after months or years. Other species lay eggs that grow into young frogs without a free-living tadpole stage.

MATING GRASP
To mate, the male frog grasps the female firmly around the body.

EGGS APLENTY
Two moor frogs mate in a pond, where lots of eggs are floating on the water's surface. This European species often mates in large groups.

The male clasps the female and hangs on until she lays her eggs. He then releases his sperm onto them.

A FROG'S STORY
The European common frog has a life cycle typical of most frogs.

On contact with the water, the jelly that surrounds the eggs swells. The eggs float in large masses near the surface.

Metamorphosis is complete at about six weeks. The young frog leaves the water, switching from a vegetarian diet to one of mainly insects.

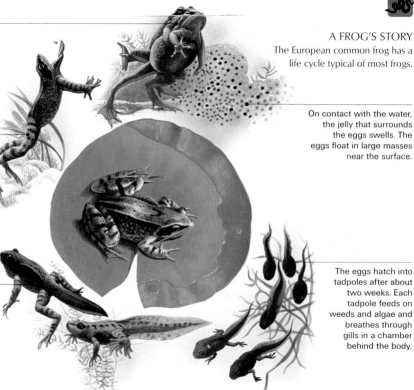

The eggs hatch into tadpoles after about two weeks. Each tadpole feeds on weeds and algae and breathes through gills in a chamber behind the body.

The lungs begin to function and the gills disappear after about three weeks. After four weeks the tail begins to shrink as the limbs gradually appear.

Caring for Eggs and Tadpoles

After laying eggs, most frogs have nothing more to do with their young. But some species take an active role in caring for their eggs and tadpoles. Some poison frogs feed their tadpoles. Females of the South American marsupial frog carry eggs on their back or in a pouch, like kangaroos. The female Australian gastric-brooding frog swallows fertilized eggs. The eggs hatch in her stomach, where the tadpoles grow into frogs.

Female carries the tadpole to a water-filled bromeliad.

After six weeks, the young frog emerges.

A MOTHER'S DUTIES
The female strawberry poison frog lays her eggs in leaf litter. When the eggs hatch, she carries the tadpoles on her back to tiny pools formed by rainwater in bromeliad plants. She returns regularly to each plant to lay unfertilized eggs in the water as food for her young.

FATHER'S SAFE HAVEN

Darwin's frogs lay their eggs on land.
When the tadpoles hatch, the male
picks them up in his mouth. They
grow into young frogs in his vocal sac.

Camouflage and Defense

Frogs' predators include snakes, birds, bats, turtles, crocodilians, fish, and other frogs. Staying hidden is one way to avoid danger—a camouflaged, still frog is very hard to spot. Running away is another—a frog can escape a predator with one or two hops. Other defenses include poisonous or bad-tasting secretions, playing dead, and puffing up the body to make the frog look larger.

LOOKS LIKE A LEAF
The Asian horned toad lives on the rain forest floor, where its shape and "dead-leaf" coloration make it almost invisible among the leaf litter.

FULL OF HOT AIR
The red-banded crevice creeper puffs its body up with air to warn off would-be predators. This species lives amongst rocks in southern Africa.

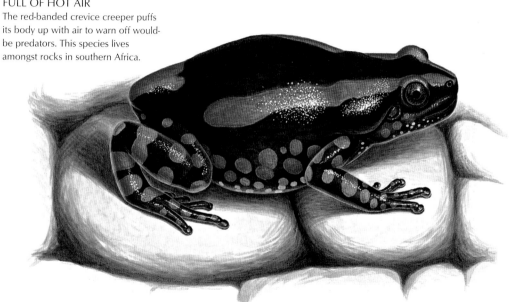

Frog Calls

Frog calls vary from faint underwater chirpings to sounds that resemble an electric buzzer or the low moan of a cow. Males make these sounds to attract females ready to mate and to warn other males to stay away from their territory. Each frog species has a unique call to which only members of that species react. A frog calls by forcing air from its lungs through the larynx, or voice box, causing the vocal cords to vibrate and produce sound. The sound is made louder by pouches of skin under, or at the corner of, the mouth.

CUTTING IN

Large males attract more females because they make louder calls than small males. This small male natterjack toad has positioned himself near a larger male, hoping to intercept females attracted by the larger male's calls.

258

CALLING FOR A MATE
This male frog calls to attract a female. Inflating the pouch of skin beneath his mouth makes the call louder than it would otherwise be.

What Frogs Eat

Relatively few frogs are large enough to eat other vertebrates, so most of them feed on insects and other arthropods, and earthworms. Some of the larger ones can take birds and mice, small turtles and fish, young snakes, and frogs of their own and other species. Frogs use their long, sticky tongue to capture small prey. Most species simply sit and wait for prey to come within reach, but some ambush their prey from hiding places.

FEARSOME PREDATOR
A large bullfrog makes a meal of the smaller carpenter frog. Apart from other frogs, bullfrogs prey on a range of animals, including birds, small mammals, and reptiles.

EAT AND BE EATEN
The South American bullfrog eats a variety of small invertebrates. In some parts of the USA, this species is itself often eaten by humans—the hind leg is served up as "mountain chicken."

Legs and Feet

Long hind legs give a frog the power it needs to jump forward.
The bones of the front legs are reinforced to absorb the shock
of landing. There are four toes on the front legs and five on the
hind legs. The shape of the toes varies depending on a frog's
lifestyle. The spadefoot toad has a spadelike growth on its hind
legs to aid in digging, while flying frogs have huge webbed
hands and feet, enabling them to glide.

EQUIPPED FOR CLIMBING
Toads are generally short-legged,
ground-dwelling animals, but
the Asiatic climbing toad
is a tree dweller with
long, slender limbs
and toe pads.

TOE TYPES
A frog's toes reflect its habits: fully
webbed for swimming; toe pads
for climbing; or claws for digging.

CLINGING ON
The tips of this tree frog's toes have
adhesive pads that help it climb trees
and cling to leaves and branches.

Frogs under the Ground

Some frogs and toads spend most of their time below the ground. These species have a spadelike growth on the inner edge of each hind foot. They use these to scoop out soil and bury themselves quickly in soft dirt or mud. A few frogs burrow head-first into the ground, and one or two dig with their front feet. A number of species encase themselves in a cocoon, which protects them from drying out while underground.

HIGH-ALTITUDE BURROWER
The colorful corroboree frog lives in burrows in bogs and marshes at altitudes above 5,000 feet (1,500 m) in the Australian Alps.

TOAD IN THE HOLE
The crucifix toad has a "spade" on each hind foot that it uses to dig into loose soil. It is seldom seen above ground except after heavy rain.

Frogs in the Trees

Many frogs are adapted to living in trees. Adhesive toe pads enable them to cling to tree trunks, and their slender body shape and long limbs allow them to leap from one leaf or branch to another. Some tree-dwelling frogs can grasp branches with their feet, like monkeys. Flying frogs have large, fully webbed feet. With the toes spread apart, the feet become parachutes and the frogs can glide from branch to branch or down to the ground.

LIFE IN THE TREES
The glass frog is a small tree dweller that inhabits the rain forests of Central and South America.

FLYING FROG

The Wallace's flying frog has broad webs of skin between the toes, allowing it to parachute between trees or guiding it in a gentle fall.

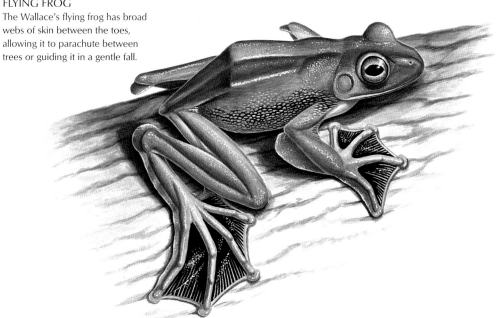

Poison Frogs

Some of the most colorful of all amphibians are the poison frogs of Central and South America. Their bright hues and striking patterns are a warning that their skin glands secrete poisons. One species is so poisonous that it is unsafe to handle it; even a small amount of poison could be fatal. These frogs are lively little foragers, with a diet consisting mainly of ants.

DID YOU KNOW?

Colombian Indians use poison frogs' secretions to coat their blow-gun darts.

COLORFUL ADVERTISING
Bright colors let predators know that they should keep well clear of the funereal poison frog.

LITTLE BEAUTY

The strawberry poison frog is beautifully colored, with a bright red body and blue limbs. Like other poison frogs, it is very small, only ½–2 inches (13–50 mm) long.

Disastrous Introductions

The cane toad is native to the Americas, from southern Texas to northern South America. In 1935 it was introduced to Australia to control beetles in sugarcane plantations. The result was a disaster. The toads bred quickly and spread, preying on native animals. Potential predators, such as snakes, can die from attempting to eat the toads, which have poison glands. Another disastrous introduction is the bullfrog, native to eastern North America. It eats and competes with local frogs wherever it has been introduced.

BULLY OF THE POND
The North American bullfrog is a fast-breeding predator with a big appetite. It is blamed for causing the extinction of native frogs in areas where it has been introduced.

CANE TOAD POISON
When cane toads are threatened, they begin sweating a milky, poisonous liquid from glands behind the eyes. The poison can be squirted quite a distance at an attacker.

KINDS OF AMPHIBIANS

Salamanders and Newts

MUDPUPPY

The mudpuppy's bushy red gills are its most prominent feature. It spends all its time in water—in rivers, streams, lakes, and ponds. Females guard their eggs.

FAST FACTS

Class: Amphibia
Order: Caudata
Family: Proteidae
Scientific name:
Necturus maculosus
Diet: Insects, crayfish, fish
Location: North America

CONGO EEL

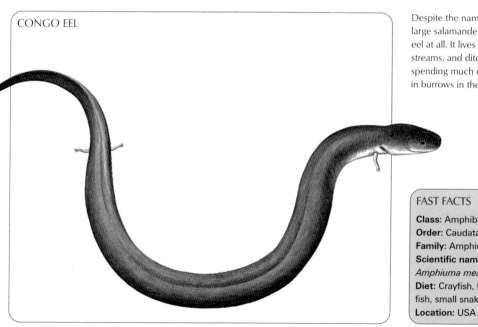

Despite the name, this large salamander is not an eel at all. It lives in swamps, streams, and ditches, spending much of its time in burrows in the mud.

FAST FACTS

Class: Amphibia
Order: Caudata
Family: Amphiumidae
Scientific name:
Amphiuma means
Diet: Crayfish, frogs, fish, small snakes
Location: USA

Salamanders and Newts

SPOTTED SALAMANDER

Like other members of the mole salamander family, this species spends its day underground, emerging at night to feed. During the breeding season, it makes its way to ponds and lakes to mate.

FAST FACTS

Class: Amphibia
Order: Caudata
Family: Ambystomatidae
Scientific name: *Ambystoma maculatum*
Diet: Earthworms, insects, spiders
Location: North America

AXOLOTL

Axolotls do not undergo metamorphosis. Even as adults, they retain gills and a tail. They are usually muddy gray in color, but some are albinos.

FAST FACTS

Class: Amphibia
Order: Caudata
Family: Ambystomatidae
Scientific name: *Ambystoma mexicanum*
Diet: Earthworms, insects, spiders, tadpoles, frogs
Location: Mexico

Salamanders and Newts

COMMON NEWT
This is how a male common newt looks for most of the year. Males develop a wavy crest from head to tail during the short breeding season, when they live in ponds with the females.

FAST FACTS

Class: Amphibia
Order: Caudata
Family: Salamandridae
Scientific name:
Triturus vulgaris
Diet: Earthworms, insects, slugs, crustaceans
Location: Europe

ALPINE NEWT

Alpine newts live in forests in mountainous or hilly areas of Europe. During the breeding season, the male (shown here) develops a low, spotted crest along its tail and back.

FAST FACTS

Class: Amphibia
Order: Caudata
Family: Salamandridae
Scientific name:
Trituris alpestris
Diet: Earthworms,
insects, slugs,
crustaceans
Location: Europe

Salamanders and Newts

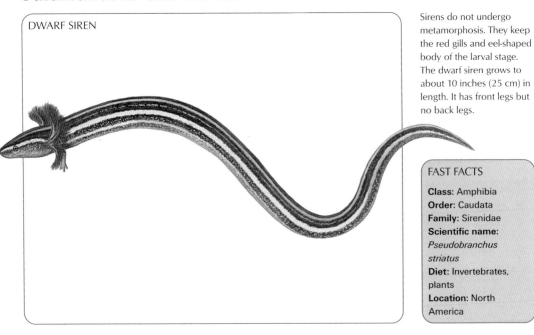

DWARF SIREN

Sirens do not undergo metamorphosis. They keep the red gills and eel-shaped body of the larval stage. The dwarf siren grows to about 10 inches (25 cm) in length. It has front legs but no back legs.

FAST FACTS

Class: Amphibia
Order: Caudata
Family: Sirenidae
Scientific name:
Pseudobranchus striatus
Diet: Invertebrates, plants
Location: North America

SLIMY SALAMANDER

The 8 inch (20 cm) slimy salamander lives on forest floors in the eastern USA. When touched, it secretes a milky gluelike substance from skin glands.

FAST FACTS

Class: Amphibia
Order: Caudata
Family: Plethodontidae
Scientific name:
Plethodon glutinosus
Diet: Earthworms, insects, slugs, other invertebrates
Location: USA

Frogs and Toads

BURROWING TREE FROG

This tree frog does not live in trees but spends much of its life underground. It has a shovel-shaped head for burrowing and, unlike other tree frogs, has no toe pads.

FAST FACTS

Class: Amphibia
Order: Anura
Family: Hylidae
Scientific name:
Pternohyla fodiens
Diet: Insects, other small invertebrates
Location: North America

GRAY TREE FROG

With skin that resembles lichen, the gray tree frog is beautifully camouflaged when it rests on a tree. It is about 2 inches (5 cm) in length and has a short broad head and stout body.

FAST FACTS

Class: Amphibia
Order: Anura
Family: Hylidae
Scientific name:
Hyla versicolor
Diet: Insects
Location: North America

RED-EYED TREE FROG

Its vivid red eyes with vertical pupils make this a distinctive species. Females lay their green eggs on vegetation or rocks overhanging ponds. The tadpoles hatch and drop into the water to complete their development.

FAST FACTS

Class: Amphibia
Order: Anura
Family: Hylidae
Scientific name:
Agalychnis callidryas
Diet: Insects, other small invertebrates
Location: Central America

Frogs and Toads

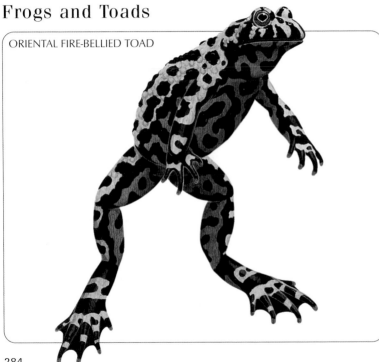

ORIENTAL FIRE-BELLIED TOAD

When disturbed, this species throws up its limbs, revealing the brightly colored underside—a warning to predators that the toad's skin secretions taste nasty.

EUROPEAN PAINTED FROG

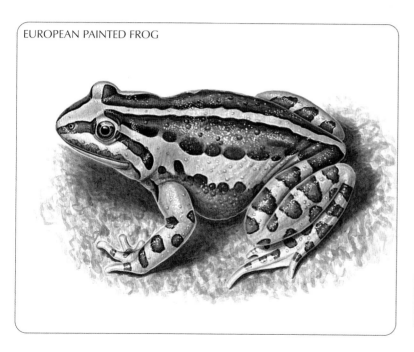

The European painted frog can often be seen sitting in shallow pools with its head just above water. It cannot extend its tongue to catch prey so instead lunges forward and grabs it with its mouth.

FAST FACTS

Class: Amphibia
Order: Anura
Family: Discoglossidae
Scientific name:
Discoglossus pictus
Diet: Insects, spiders, other invertebrates
Location: Europe

Frogs and Toads

MEXICAN BURROWING TOAD

This toad spends most of its life underground, emerging only to breed after heavy rain. On the inner edge of each hind foot is a "spade," which the toad uses to dig as it shuffles backward into the soil.

FAST FACTS

Class: Amphibia
Order: Anura
Family: Rhinophrynidae
Scientific name:
Rhinophrynus dorsalis
Diet: Ants, termites
Location: North and Central America

CAPE CLAWED FROG

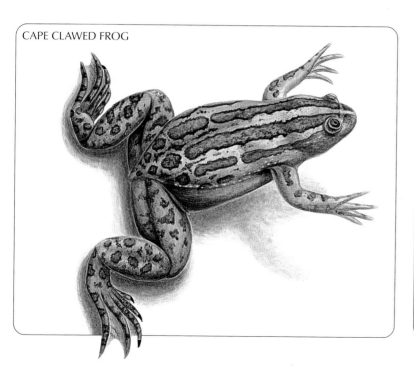

Like other clawed frogs, this species has a flattened body, powerful legs, and large, fully webbed feet with three clawlike toes. It has no tongue and relies heavily on its front feet to catch food.

FAST FACTS

Class: Amphibia
Order: Anura
Family: Pipidae
Scientific name:
Xenopus gilli
Diet: Arthropods, fish, amphibians
Location: South Africa

Frogs and Toads

COUCH'S SPADEFOOT TOAD

All spadefoot toads have a spadelike structure on each hind foot. They use this to dig rapidly backward, circling as they descend. They spend the day—most of the year if rain is scarce—in their deep burrows.

FAST FACTS

Class: Amphibia
Order: Anura
Family: Pelobatidae
Scientific name:
Scaphiopus couchii
Diet: Insects, other arthropods
Location: North America

WESTERN BARKING FROG

This frog has earned its common name from the noise it makes—a short, sharp, throaty sound uttered every two or three seconds that resembles the barking of a dog. It often hides by day in caves and crevices or down wells.

FAST FACTS

Class: Amphibia
Order: Anura
Family: Leptodactylidae
Scientific name:
Eleutherodactylus augusti
Diet: Insects, other arthropods
Location: North America

Frogs and Toads

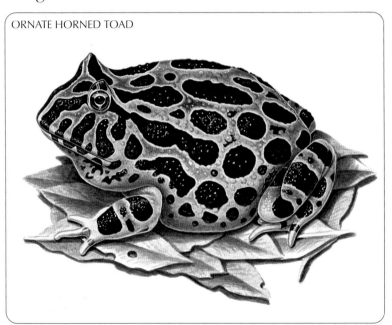

ORNATE HORNED TOAD

The ornate horned toad is an aggressive predator with a very wide mouth. It cannot move quickly, so lies partially buried among leaf litter on the rain forest floor and ambushes its prey. It eats almost anything it can swallow.

FAST FACTS

Class: Amphiba
Order: Anura
Family: Leptodactylidae
Scientific name:
Ceratophrys ornata
Diet: Insects, frogs, lizards, snakes, small mammals
Location: Argentina

SPOTTED GRASS FROG

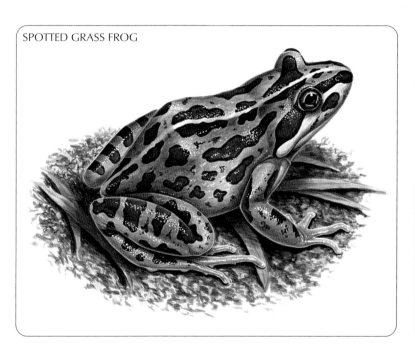

This species is usually found in marshy areas or near streams and ponds with grassy edges. During the day it sits under stones, fallen timber, and debris close to the water's edge.

FAST FACTS

Class: Amphiba
Order: Anura
Family: Myobatrachidae
Scientific name: *Limnodynastes tasmaniensis*
Diet: Insects, other invertebrates
Location: Australia

Frogs and Toads

VARIABLE HARLEQUIN FROG

The strong colors of this frog are its most distinctive feature. The colors are a warning to potential predators that the frog's skin secretes powerful poisons.

FAST FACTS

Class: Amphibia
Order: Anura
Family: Bufonidae
Scientific name:
Atelopus varius
Diet: Insects, other invertebrates
Location: South and Central America

LEOPARD TOAD

The leopard toad is a ground dweller that hides during the day, usually in holes. It comes out at night to hop about looking for prey, which it snaps up with its long, sticky tongue.

FAST FACTS

Class: Amphibia
Order: Anura
Family: Bufonidae
Scientific name:
Bufo pardalis
Diet: Insects, other invertebrates
Location: Africa

Frogs and Toads

GREEN AND GOLD BELL FROG

Active by night and day, this frog enjoys basking in the sun near ponds, swamps, and streams, slipping into the water to cool off when necessary. It catches its prey by lunging forward and seizing it with both front feet.

FAST FACTS

Class: Amphibia
Order: Anura
Family: Hylidae
Scientific name:
Litoria aurea
Diet: Invertebrates, frogs, snakes
Location: Australia

BLUE POISON FROG

Like other poison frogs, this species lays its eggs in moist, sheltered places on land. The males guard the eggs. When the eggs hatch, the tadpoles wriggle onto the male's back and are carried to water.

FAST FACTS

Class: Amphibia
Order: Anura
Family: Dendrobatidae
Scientific name:
Dendrobates azureus
Diet: Ants
Location: Suriname

Frogs and Toads

WOOD FROG

The wood frog has very long legs and is a powerful jumper. When it keeps still, this frog is almost invisible because its brown and gray coloring blends in so well with the forest floor.

FAST FACTS

Class: Amphibia
Order: Anura
Family: Ranidae
Scientific name: *Rana sylvatica*
Diet: Insects, snails, other invertebrates
Location: North America

PICKEREL FROG

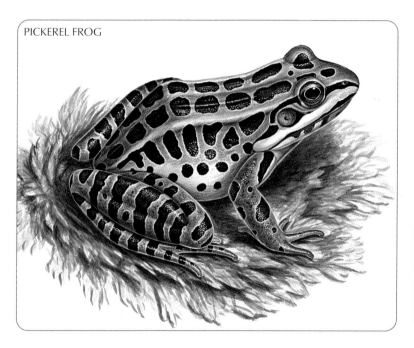

The pickerel frog lives in and around brooks and streams, spending more time out of water than in it. It produces a poisonous skin secretion that irritates human skin and can kill small animals.

FAST FACTS

Class: Amphibia
Order: Anura
Family: Ranidae
Scientific name: *Rana palustris*
Diet: Insects, snails, crustaceans
Location: North America

Endangered Reptiles and Amphibians

Threats to reptiles and amphibians include habitat destruction, hunting for meat and for the pet trade, and competition from introduced animals. Amphibians are especially at risk: being in such close contact with air, water, and soil, they are the first animals to be hit if something is wrong. Frog populations have declined dramatically since the 1970s. Pollution, pesticides, and global warming may be to blame.

CHEMICALS AND DEFORMITIES
Chemical pollution in ponds caused this frog to develop extra legs. Frogs and other amphibians are at great risk from chemicals.

FIJIAN CRESTED IGUANA
This iguana is nearly extinct because of habitat destruction and being eaten by introduced species.

AMAZON RIVER TURTLE
The yellow-spotted Amazon River turtle is endangered due to hunting for its meat and eggs.

INDIGO SNAKE
Loss of habitat and collection for the pet trade endanger this snake.

BACK FROM THE DEAD
The Australian pygmy blue-tongue skink had not been seen for 33 years when, in 1992, one was discovered in a dead snake. Live populations of the skink were found, but it is very rare.

Classifying Reptiles and Amphibians

The way in which reptiles and amphibians are classified is constantly changing, and the most recent system is given below.

CLASS AMPHIBIA

Subclass Lissamphibia

ORDER CAUDATA
SALAMANDERS & NEWTS

Suborder	**Sirenoidea**
Sirenidae	Sirens

Suborder	**Cryptobranchoidea**
Cryptobranchidae	Hellbenders & Giant Salamanders
Hynobiidae	Hynobiids

Suborder	**Salamandroidea**
Amphiumidae	Amphiumas (Congo Eels)
Plethodontidae	Lungless Salamanders
Rhyacotritonidae	Torrent Salamanders
Proteidae	Mudpuppies, Waterdogs, & The Olm
Salamandridae	Salamandrids
Ambystomatidae	Mole Salamanders
Dicamptodontidae	Dicamptodontids

ORDER GYMNOPHIONA
CAECILIANS

Rhinatrematidae	South American Tailed Caecilians
Ichthyophiidae	Ichthyophiids
Uraeotyphlidae	Uraeotyphlids
Scolecomorphidae	Scolecomorphids
Caeciliidae	Caeciliids & Aquatic Caecilians

ORDER ANURA
FROGS & TOADS

Suborder	**Archaeobatrachia**
Ascaphidae	"Tailed" Frogs
Leiopelmatidae	New Zealand Frogs
Bombinatoridae	Fire-Bellied Toads & Allies
Discoglossidae	Discoglossid Frogs
Pipidae	Pipas & "Clawed" Frogs
Rhinophrynidae	Cone-Nosed Frog
Megophryidae	Megophryids
Pelodytidae	Parsley Frogs
Pelobatidae	Spadefoots

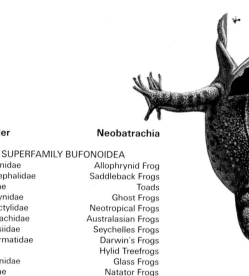

Suborder

Neobatrachia

SUPERFAMILY BUFONOIDEA

Allophrynidae	Allophrynid Frog
Brachycephalidae	Saddleback Frogs
Bufonidae	Toads
Helophrynidae	Ghost Frogs
Leptodactylidae	Neotropical Frogs
Myobatrachidae	Australasian Frogs
Sooglossiidae	Seychelles Frogs
Rhinodermatidae	Darwin's Frogs
Hylidae	Hylid Treefrogs
Centrolenidae	Glass Frogs
Pseudidae	Natator Frogs
Dendrobatidae	Dart-Poison Frogs

SUPERFAMILY RANOIDEA

Microhylidae	Microhylids
Hemisotidae	Shovel-Nosed Frogs
Arthroleptidae	Squeakers
Ranidae	Ranid Frogs
Hyperoliidae	Reed & Lily Frogs
Rhacophoridae	Rhacaphorid Treefrogs

Million years ago

208	144	65	2	
JURASSIC	CRETACEOUS	PALEOCENE EOCENE	OLIGOCENE MIOCENE	PLIOCENE PLEISTOCENE PRESENT

ASCAPHUS

LEIOPELMA

BOMBINATORIDAE

DISCOGLOSSIDAE

MEGOPHRYIDAE

PELOBATIDAE

PELODYTIDAE

RHINOPHRYNIDAE

PIPIDAE

NEOBATRACHIA

CLASS REPTILIA

Subclass Eureptilia

SUPERORDER LEPIDOSAURIA

ORDER RHYNCHOCEPHALIA
TUATARAS

Sphenodontidae   Tuataras

ORDER SQUAMATA
SQUAMATES

Suborder Iguania	**Iguanid Lizards**
Corytophanidae	Helmeted Lizards
Crotaphytidae	Collared & Leopard Lizards
Hoplocercidae	Hoplocercids
Iguanidae	Iguanas
Opluridae	Madagascar Iguanians
Phrynosomatidae	Scaly, Sand & Horned Lizards
Polychrotidae	Anoloid Lizards
Tropiduridae	Tropidurids
Agamidae	Agamid Lizards
Chameleonidae	Chameleons

Suborder Scleroglossa

SUPERFAMILY GEKKONOIDEA

Eublepharidae	Eye-Lash Geckos
Gekkonidae	Geckos
Pygopodidae	Australasian Flapfoots

SUPERFAMILY SCINCOIDEA

Xantusiidae	Night Lizards
Lacertidae	Lacertids
Scincidae	Skinks
Dibamidae	Dibamids
Cordylidae	Girdle-Tailed Lizards
Gerrhosauridae	Plated Lizards
Teiidae	Macroteiids
Gymnophthalmidae	Microteiids

SUPERFAMILY ANGUOIDEA

Xenosauridae	Knob-Scaled Lizards
Anguidae	Anguids; Glass & Alligator Lizards
Helodermatidae	Beaded Lizards
Varanidae	Monitor Lizards
Lanthanotidae	Earless Monitor Lizard

Suborder Amphisbaenia

Amphisbaenians

Bipedidae	Ajolotes
Amphisbaenidae	Worm Lizards
Trogonophidae	Desert Ringed Lizards
Rhineuridae	Florida Worm Lizard

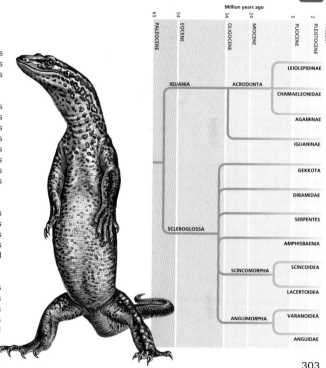

Suborder Serpentes   Snakes

Infraorder	**Scolecophidia**
Anomalepididae	Blind Wormsnakes
Typhlopidae	Blind Snakes
Leptotyphlopidae	Thread Snakes

Infraorder	**Alethinophidia**
Anomochelidae	Stump Heads
Aniliidae	Coral Pipesnakes
Cylindrophidae	Asian Pipesnakes
Uropeltidae	Shield Tails
Xenopeltidae	Sunbeam Snake
Loxocemidae	Dwarf Boa
Boidae	Pythons & Boas
Ungaliophiidae	Ungaliophiids
Bolyeriidae	Round Island Snakes
Tropidophiidae	Woodsnakes
Acrochordidae	File Snakes
Atractaspididae	Mole Vipers
Colubridae	Harmless & Rear-Fanged Snakes
Elapidae	Cobras, Kraits, Coral Snakes & Sea Snakes
Viperidae	Adders & Vipers

SUPERORDER TESTUDINES

ORDER TESTUDINATA
TURTLES, TERRAPINS & TORTOISES

Suborder Pleurodira	**Side-Neck Turtles**
Chelidae	Snake-Neck Turtles
Pelomedusidae	Helmeted Side-Neck Turtles

Suborder Cryptodira
                 Hidden-Necked Turtles

SUPERFAMILY TRIONYCHOIDEA

Kinosternidae	Mud & Musk Turtles
Dermatemydidae	Mesoamerican River Turtle
Carretochelyidae	Australian Softshell Turtle
Trionychidae	Holarctic & Paleotropical Softshell Turtles

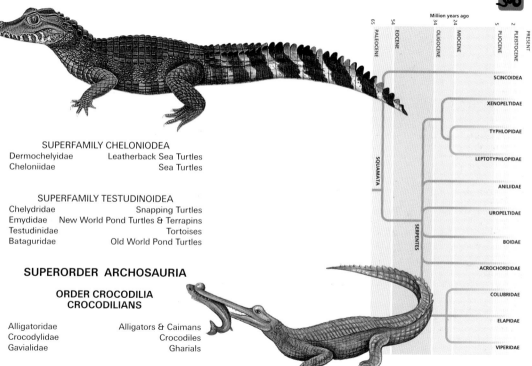

Million years ago

PALEOCENE	EOCENE	OLIGOCENE	MIOCENE	PLIOCENE	PLEISTOCENE	PRESENT
65	54	34	24	5	2	

SCINCOIDEA

XENOPELTIDAE

TYPHLOPIDAE

LEPTOTYPHLOPIDAE

ANILIIDAE

UROPELTIDAE

BOIDAE

ACROCHORDIDAE

COLUBRIDAE

ELAPIDAE

VIPERIDAE

SQUAMATA

SERPENTES

SUPERFAMILY CHELONIODEA
Dermochelyidae   Leatherback Sea Turtles
Cheloniidae   Sea Turtles

SUPERFAMILY TESTUDINOIDEA
Chelydridae   Snapping Turtles
Emydidae   New World Pond Turtles & Terrapins
Testudinidae   Tortoises
Bataguridae   Old World Pond Turtles

SUPERORDER ARCHOSAURIA

ORDER CROCODILIA
CROCODILIANS

Alligatoridae   Alligators & Caimans
Crocodylidae   Crocodiles
Gavialidae   Gharials

Glossary

adaptation A change that occurs in an animal's behavior or body form to allow it to survive and breed in new conditions.

amphibian A vertebrate that can live on land and in water. Amphibians (frogs and toads, salamanders and newts, and caecilians) are similar to reptiles, but they have moist skin and they lay their eggs in water.

aquatic Living in water all or most of the time.

arboreal Living in trees all or most of the time.

arthropod An animal with jointed legs and a hard external skeleton. Insects, spiders, crustaceans, centipedes, and millipedes are all arthropods.

bask To hold the body in a position directly exposed to the sun's rays.

camouflage The colors and patterns of an animal that enable it to blend in with the background.

carapace The upper part of a chelonian's shell.

carnivore An animal that eats only meat.

chelonian A turtle or tortoise. A member of the order Chelonia.

cocoon In amphibians, a case made of mud, mucus, or similar material, in which the animal rests.

courtship The behavior of animals that ultimately results in mating.

crest In lizards, a line of large, scaly spines on the neck and back.

crocodilian A crocodile, alligator, caiman, or gharial. A member of the order Crocodilia.

crustacean A mostly aquatic animal, such as a lobster, crab, or prawn, that has a hard external skeleton.

dewlap In a lizard, a flap of skin on the throat.

display Behavior used by an animal to communicate with its own species, or with other animals. Displays, which include postures, actions, or showing brightly colored parts of the body, may signal threat, defense, or readiness to mate.

ectothermic Unable to keep the body at a stable, warm temperature by internal means. Reptiles and amphibians are ectothermic but maintain a high body temperature by behavior, for example by basking in the sun.

embryo An unborn animal in the earliest stages of development.

endangered In danger of becoming extinct.

endothermic Able to regulate body temperature by internal means, regardless of the outside temperature. Birds and mammals are endothermic.

environment All the natural features of Earth, such as landforms and climate, that affect living things.

evolution The gradual change in plants and animals, over many generations, in response to their environment.

extinct Of a species, no longer in existence.

frill A collar around a lizard's neck.

gastroliths Stones swallowed by animals such as crocodilians, that stay in the stomach and help crush food.

gill An organ that absorbs oxygen from water.

habitat The place where an animal naturally lives. Many different kinds of animals live in the same environment, but each kind lives in a different habitat within that environment.

hatchling A young animal, such as a bird or reptile, that has recently hatched from its egg.

herbivore An animal that eats only plant material, such as leaves.

invertebrate An animal that does not have a backbone. Many invertebrates are soft-bodied animals, but most, such as insects, have a hard external skeleton.

larva (plural larvae) A young animal that looks completely different from its parents. In amphibians, the larval stage is the stage before metamorphosis that breathes with gills rather than lungs (for example, tadpoles).

metamorphosis A way of development in which an animal's body changes shape over a short period of time. Amphibians undergo metamorphosis as they grow to maturity.

mimicry A strategy by which an animal copies or imitates another animal, either to hunt or to avoid being hunted.

neoteny The retention by an animal of some immature or larval characteristics into adulthood.

plastron The lower part of a chelonian's shell.

predator An animal that hunts or preys on other animals for its food.

prey An animal that is hunted by predators.

reptile An ectothermic vertebrate with dry, scaly skin. Tortoises, turtles, snakes, lizards, and crocodilians are reptiles.

scales In reptiles, thickened areas of skin that vary in size.

scutes In chelonians, the horny plates that cover the bony shell.

species A group of animals with very similar features that are able to breed together and produce fertile young.

tadpole The larva of a frog or toad. Tadpoles live in water and take in oxygen through gills.

temperate Describes a region or environment that has a warm (but not very hot) summer and a cool (but not very cold) winter.

territory An area of land inhabited by an animal and defended by it.

toxin Poisonous substance produced by a plant or animal.

tropical Describes a region or environment near the Equator that is warm to hot all year round.

venom Poison injected by animals into a predator or prey through fangs, spines, or similar structures.

venomous Describes an animal that delivers a venom.

vertebrate An animal with a backbone—an internal skeleton of cartilage or bone. Fish, reptiles, birds, amphibians, and mammals are all vertebrates.

Index

Acknowledgments

PHOTOGRAPHIC CREDITS

Key t=top; l=left; r=right; tl=top left; tcl=top center left; tc=top center; tcr=top center right; tr=top right; cl=center left; c=center; cr=center right; b=bottom; bl=bottom left; bcl=bottom center left; bc=bottom center; bcr=bottom center right; br=bottom right

AUS = Auscape International; CBCD = Corbis CD; COR = Corel Corp. DV = Digital Vision; iS = istockphoto.com; PD = Photodisc; PE = PhotoEssentials; PL = photolibrary.com

19c COR **21**c iS **43**c COR **47**l iS **48**l, r COR **49**c COR **50**r COR **53**c PD **56**l COR **74**b iS **79**br COR **81**c COR **83**c COR **91**c COR **100**br iS **101**c PD **102**br COR **104**l, r COR **107**c DV **115**c PE **118**bl PL **121**c COR **125**t PL **131**c COR **135**l COR **136**br iS **137**c PL **149**c COR **155**c COR **157**c COR **170**l COR **191**c COR **197**c COR **217**c COR **227**c COR **229**c COR **230**bl COR **238**br COR **239**c COR **241**c iS **246**bl PL **249**c AUS **252**bl iS **261**c CBCD **263**c COR **271**c COR **276**cl COR **277**cl PL **278**cl iS **282**tr iS **283**cl COR **295**cl iS **296**cl COR

ILLUSTRATION CREDITS

Alistar Barnard, Anne Bowman, Barbara Rodanska, Christer Eriksson, Colin Newman/Bernard Thornton Artists UK, David Kirshner, Fiammetta Dogi, Frank Knight, James McKinnon, John Francis/Bernard Thornton Artists UK, Jon Gittoes, Ken Oliver/The Art Agency, Kevin Stead, Map Illustrations, MagicGroup s.r.o (Czech Republic)— www.magicgroup.cz, Peter Schouten, Rob Mancini, Robert Hynes, Rod Westblade, Roger Swainston, Simone End, Tony Pyrzakowski, Trevor Ruth

INDEX

Puddingburn Publishing Services

CONSULTANT

Dr Mark Hutchinson is the Researcher in Herpetology at the South Australian Museum, where he has worked since 1990. His research has included studies of reptile and amphibian biology and evolution, the classification and evolution of Australian lizards, and the distribution and conservation of reptiles in Australia.